On
Becoming
POWERFUL

D0011870

On Becoming POWERFUL

John Volkmar

SAMUEL WEISER, INC.
York Beach, Maine

First published in 1988 by
Samuel Weiser, Inc.
Box 612
York Beach, Maine 03910

Library of Congress Cataloging in Publication Data

Volkmar, John.
    On becoming powerful / John Volkmar
      p. cm.
    ISBN 0-87728-676-0
    1. Self-actualization (Psychology) 2. Control (Psychology).
3. Success. 4. Visualization. 5. Meditation.
6. Cerebral dominance. I. Title.

BF637.S4V65 1988
158'.1--dc19   88-20582
                                                CIP

Cover mandala is entitled "Cultural Montage" © 1988 by Jeanette
Stobie. Ms. Stobie, an artist from Redwood City, California, says of
this image: "As I painted, I was hoping to reflect the sense of
chronological time—represented by the four flames burning
throughout evolutionary history across cultures, religions and
creativity—being juxtaposed against the ever-present eternal time,
represented by the lotus center."

Typeset in 11 point Palatino

Printed in the United States of America

To my wonderful soulmate, Joanne, who has given me an enormous amount of encouragement and support and, above all, unconditional love during illness. A word of gratitude to all the individuals who have trusted me with their deepest feelings.

Contents

Foreword xi

About the Author xv

Introduction xvii

Chapter 1: First Steps 1

Chapter 2: Getting a Grip on Stress 9

Chapter 3: Managing Stress in Your Life 23

Chapter 4: Making Visualization Work for You 37

Chapter 5: Using Your Spirit Guide 43

Chapter 6: Developing Your Psychic Tools 47

Chapter 7: Life Energy and Thought Forms 55

Chapter 8: Ego Trips and Traps 69

Chapter 9: Using the Mandala and *I-Ching* 73

Chapter 10: Healing Opportunities 81

Chapter 11: Functions of the Counselor/Healer 95

Chapter 12: On With the Healing 107

Afterword: A Beginning 121

List of Exercises

Exercise 1. Energizing Breath 2

Exercise 2. Letting Go 3

Exercise 3. Who Am I? 3

Exercise 4. Cleansing the Memory Bank 6

Exercise 5. Alpha One 26

Exercise 6. Inner Tranquility 28

Exercise 7. Granted Favors 39

Exercise 8. Meeting Your Spirit Guide 45

Exercise 9. Opening the Channel 49

Exercise 10. Focusing 50

Exercise 11. Take a Trip 51

Exercise 12. Sea Sounds 51

Exercise 13. Controlled Blinking 52

Exercise 14. Imposing on the Right Brain 53

Exercise 15.   Giant to Dwarf 54

Exercise 16.   Integration 57

Exercise 17.   First Look at Energy Fields 58

Exercise 18.   The Plant Aura 59

Exercise 19.   Psychometry 61

Exercise 20.   Aura Reading 66

Exercise 21.   Creating Your Mandala 76

Exercise 22.   Working with the *I-Ching* 78

Exercise 23.   Chakra Scanning 85

Exercise 24.   Sufi Color Meditation 88

Exercise 25.   Forgiveness 103

Exercise 26.   I Love You 105

Foreword

It may seem at first contradictory that a man who has spent his life making peace would write a book on how to become powerful. One tends to associate power with the raised fist or, more subtly, the steely glint of an eye—he who wields unbending control over others. How would a career as negotiator on sensitive peace missions in foreign service lay the foundation for a book on *power*? To answer this, we have to redefine and altogether rethink what real power means.

It came to me—the whole gist of what it means to be truly powerful—with John Volkmar, in fact. We were sitting on my terrace talking about his book. I said "Someone will have to write a foreword for this book—it's a gem." He looked at me earnestly and asked, "Well, *would* you?" I smiled. "So that's power," I thought.

What made John's gesture powerful rather than manipulative is that he had intuitively recognized a *common* need between us: his to get a preface written, and mine to write it. Writing is therapeutic for me; I was feeling terribly stressed and this particular project would channel my energies. Of course I would do the preface.

The book is, after all, about methods of meditation that relax and focus you, as well as heighten your powers of intuition. But it is no ordinary manual of skills. It was designed just for me, yet for you, also, for readers everywhere. Seldom have I read a book so personally evocative in style and approach. Seldom have complex ideas been so limpidly and leisurely expressed, in a manner so non-judgmental as to put me fully at my ease. It is therapy indeed! But how to convey this to the reader in a mere preface?

The most obvious quality of the book permeates the style: it makes you feel good. This is not an evanescent bubble of emotion. It refers to a state of mind, a quality of consciousness. The book believes (it assumes its own voice) that all human beings are inherently good. Without confidence in your own deep inner good you cannot be powerful. The purpose of the book is thus to teach ways of tapping that good, which is to say, soul qualities—such as nobility, patience, temperance, joy, courage, strength.

Implicit in its message is the principle that my good increases and is increased by yours; that true power means *empowerment*. Empowerment is a feminine principle which rejects the standard verticle climb to power in favor of a sweeping curve, a mode of cooperation and ever-expanding awareness which embraces and shares rather than competes. When the empowerment principle is at work, no one is victim of a role; everyone is participant in a greater whole. The book itself advances from methods of self-control and self-healing to methods of healing others. The two go hand in hand.

While the purpose of the book is to train you to tap and share your inner good—for that is how you become powerful—there is a catch. The book is meant to be *used*. It is just what it says— a handbook—dealing with a process, a becoming. Exactly what is it that you contact within yourself to make these inner changes? This book refers to a fundamental triangle of communication connecting mind, body, and spirit. This triangle forms the ancient foundation upon which holistic thinking is based. "Mind" and "spirit" have been renamed here with the familiar synonyms "left brain" and "right brain" respectively, or conscious and unconscious mind, with "body" in the center, as it were, exchanging messages with both sources. Stress originates in the right-brain, and blocks the natural flow of energy in the triangle. It is this source that you must contact in order to reduce stress and release the flow again. A corrective message must be sent to the right-brain, but the right-brain is non-verbal; it understands only images. Hence, you will learn to communicate by means of visualization.

The purpose of this handbook is to put you in touch with the higher self using specific techniques of relaxation, visualization, and the enlightened use of other important tools. You will learn how to listen actively, not passively, in order to distinguish the true voice from the false, so you can get rid of flimsy and illusory supports of comfortable old habits and social patterns. The purpose of active meditation is not to ignore or fight old patterns. It is to *replace* them with new blueprints—vivid and highly specialized mental pictures—which will invoke your soul energy to flow freely again.

In order to replace old patterns, you must learn how to recognize them. Hence this book gently ushers you toward techniques of confrontation with those secret parts of yourself wherein your weaknesses are hidden, even from yourself—anger, jealousy, fear, impatience. Once you can recognize and re-organize or at least begin to gain conscious control of your life, you will feel the difference. The result of your effort is eventual integration: a sense of inner peace, vitality and good health, prosperity, and joy. How could it be otherwise, the gentle but convincing voice of this book suggests?

Indeed, the books speaks for itself. You'll see.

——Virginia MacIvor Meyn, Ph.D.

About the Author

John Volkmar has been on a focused spiritual path since 1954, studying and experiencing the steps leading to spiritual fulfillment. Today, both as a teacher and student, he continues his search for universal truths while helping clients to take responsibility for their lives and achieve inner tranquility and a high level of wellness.

His search has taken him to many parts of the world. He and his wife Joanne organized educational and development projects in North and West Africa, the Middle East and Asia. In West Africa, the Middle East and at the United Nations he initiated and participated in peacemaking efforts between nations at war and between liberation groups and governments in power. He has written and published articles, and coauthored one book with the President of the International Peace Academy, Ret. Gen. Indar Rikhye, entitled *The Middle East and a New Realism*, published by the academy in 1975. He also wrote a book for International Documentation, Inc. in New York in 1977, called *Geneva or Elsewhere*, which made new proposals for a peace settlement in the Middle East.

The theme of his life has been to persuade individuals, communities and nations who feel powerless to develop their inherent power in order to improve their lives. In his work today as a holistic teacher with individuals and groups, the emphasis is the same: when you take responsibility for yourself physically, mentally and spiritually, then true wellness will be experienced. He teaches self-healing skills, how to avoid illness recurrence, life management, techniques for building self-esteem, and how to use creative visualization to achieve goals and develop right brain skills for more effective personal and professional life. He presently lives in Guilford, Connecticut, where he leads workshops.

Introduction

There has to be a good reason to write a book, to add another eighty thousand words to the billions that have already been printed. And there is! I want to share an exciting personal growth process with you — a process that you, too, can use to achieve real power. It would help if we could become good friends while we work together. Let's agree to that possibility as we work our way through your personal spiritual transformation during the weeks before us.

You can acquire a lifestyle that you never imagined possible by following the lessons one by one, at your own pace, and in your own style. After you have completed the exercises and are attuned to the real meaning of power of life, you will be seeking ways to share this vibrance and wisdom with others. For this reason, I offer a chapter to prepare you for the role as counselor/healer, to give you an opportunity to make a contribution to those in need and to continue on the path you have chosen.* Everyone of us knows at this moment someone who is seriously ill. What a gift you can give them by encouraging them to recognize the capacity they have to heal themselves.

We need to begin by understanding the difference between power as it is generally known and the spiritual power which this book is about. Some of us believe that to

---

*I also teach workshops and work with individuals who are ready to take charge of their lives or heal themselves of a physical, mental or spiritual illness.

be really powerful is to be able to manipulate events and people to satisfy ego and material needs. And others of us are not able to be that honest with ourselves, but at least unconsciously we are driven by the same process. We soon discover that as soon as one need is satisfied, it is followed by a creeping discontent, which we treat with another struggle for more power. A large percentage of us are caught up in this whirlpool; manipulating, buying, running up debts, double-jobbing, destroying relationships and marriages, sacrificing good health in the pursuit of symbols of power—the American Express Gold Card, Lincoln Continentals, time-sharing apartments in chic or "in" resorts, designer labeled clothes, and on and on. We treat the discontent and resultant depressions by abusing ourselves with doctor prescribed uppers and downers, or alcohol, cocaine, heroin and reefer.

Some of us are becoming aware of uncomfortable nagging questions: Is this all that life has to offer? Is this constant race the reason why we are born? Or is there perhaps some treat which is eluding us, some opportunity which we overlooked while growing up?

We all know one or two people whom we admire very much, for special hard to explain reasons. We wish we could be more like them, lead the kind of life they do. The qualities we admire in them are dominated by an aura of being in charge of their lives and environment, and even exerting a positive influence over people with whom they come in contact. They are admired by many people, and their friends are people of accomplishment and success. These friends often share the same qualities. Their value systems do not drive them to acquire things unless they are useful, and when they decide to buy something, it is always of good quality, or if they plan a trip, the money always seems to be there. They are thought to be wealthy, but actually they have learned to manage their money as well as their lives, to resist the hard sell of the advertising industry, to reduce their material needs to a reasonable minimum. They radiate a composure and inner tranquility, even an unflappability in the face of sudden change or disappointment. Amazingly, things always seem to work out for them, as if an invisible hand were assigned to preserve their unruffled life. They have discovered the meaning of prosperity.

There is nothing abnormal about these truly powerful people. Their I.Q.'s are normal, their education not necessarily of university level, their physical make-up unexceptional. What does make them exceptional is that they have learned a secret, *which is available to everyone.* They are following a program of self-help in order to achieve their power. They have dedicated a very small portion of their day to maintaining a high degree of mental, spiritual and physical wellness. The exercises they do are easy to follow and are based on principles used for thousands of years in the process of self-fulfillment and self-awareness. They cherish the time they spend for themselves and look forward to their daily exercises.

What were some of the problems they faced, which you may face, as they began to turn their lives around? The first is fear: fear of change, fear of the unknown (even though improved) future lifestyle, of giving up old crutches and cop-outs, fear of failure, or even more difficult to deal with—fear of success.

The second problem is the pain of loneliness which accompanies the chosen path of spiritual growth. You deeply feel the need to share your new experiences. Inevitably, a person who is on the same path will appear in your life and make the pain more manageable, for your new friends will know the pain of which you speak.

The third is the lack of support (or even ridicule) from friends and loved ones. You only wish that they, too, could experience the same challenges. You soon learn a simple truth: no one can force or impose personal growth and change. You learn to be content with presenting others an array of options that they may not have considered before.

The fourth is taking responsibility for the sometimes drastic changes you may decide to make: change in career, marriage partner, lifestyle and treatment of your fellow human beings. Those around you may feel hurt, left out, or rejected. This is inevitable. Compensate for their feelings with extra heavy doses of love and understanding. For these changes to be positive it is important not to feel guilty for having chosen your path.

The fifth problem comes somewhere along the early stages of the process. It is a disbelief of what is happening to you, the feeling that you are not entitled to a better life, that the sacrifices are not worth it. At this point let's hope that you will have found a kindred spirit, someone on the same path, who can reassure you and reinforce your commitment to yourself.

The sixth problem is trying to explain what is happening to you, answering questions that indicate an unawareness of the changes that are taking place in you. Find some easy-to-understand explanation, which, like a slogan, will be repeated frequently to your friends and associates. It will assuage their fears of losing you, and in some cases, the guilt they feel for not really caring.

The seventh and most difficult problem is how to deal with the set-backs, the sometimes one step backward to every two steps forward. How do you handle the frustrations of gray days when nothing seems to work for you, when your ability to focus seems to have disappeared? During those periods, to curl up and indulge yourself in the old dependencies seems *so* alluring. You may decide to take a Valium, an extra couple of martinis, buy a new dress or an electric tool that you don't need. Instead, find something to do which calls upon your creativity and ingenuity whose source is the right brain (or unconscious), which is also the source of your confusion and lack of focus. Build a shelf, bake an almond torte, repair a broken toaster or plan an exciting vacation. Above all, develop patience and be confident that in a few days the path will seem clearer and that forward movement will again be noticeable.

If this introduction has helped to reinforce your commitment to yourself, or given the impression that the program is difficult and full of hard work, it has done its job. Perhaps it has, however, neglected to emphasize the accompanying excitement and moments of joy which are also a part of the process.

CHAPTER

1

First Steps

Your goal is to become powerful. You can accomplish this by getting in touch with your higher self and, on the way, with the many layers of your personality. Some call this higher self the spiritual self or the soul: whatever the name, you can become friends with all your various parts again and feel spiritually integrated at last. This handbook will provide an easy-to-follow, self-administered program to develop spiritual power. The program utilizes your natural abilities in combination with a strong commitment to achieve your goal of personal integration.

Begin the program by finding a spot in your home where it feels good to be, and whenever you do any exercise from this book, sit there. Set a schedule which allows you to devote one-half hour per day to yourself. If necessary, wake up half an hour earlier in the morning. Don't groan. You won't feel tired at the end of the day for giving up that half hour.

Buy yourself a spiral notebook or journal, and carry it around with you wherever you go, even when you go shopping. Lots of good thinking time in a car or on a bus can produce some ideas for later use in your special spot at home. In this journal you do not need to keep track of the days; just make notes of thoughts that you don't want to forget. Don't worry about grammar—it's not going to be published. Buy an inexpensive cassette recorder/player and some blank tapes.

Announce to your family—or the people you live with—that you are beginning a self-help program and you'd like their cooperation in respecting your quiet times every day. No interruptions, please.

Now that you have your space all set and your equipment together, let's set out to find out who you are. You'll begin the process by getting in touch with the many layers of your personality and eventually with your higher self. Ask yourself, "Who am I really? What makes me different from everyone else? What are my likes and dislikes, my values? What do I truly believe in? What am I prepared to defend? How am I seen by others? Do they see me as I really am? Am I loved? Do I love?" You will work with these questions later.

EXERCISE 1
Energizing Breath

On your first morning (or evening, if that's your choice) for your half hour, sit comfortably and close your eyes. Relax your body, and start to breathe deeply and very slowly. Not too slowly, as you might get tense trying not to breathe too fast. You'll know what is comfortable for you. However, as you get into practice, you'll find that you need less oxygen when you are physically relaxed and in balance. You will also breathe less deeply and frequently. As you breathe in, feel as if energy is flowing into your body through the soles of your feet, up your legs, into your heart area, and finally to your head, making your thoughts clearer and more focused. When you exhale slowly, think of the events of the day that upset you, and watch them flowing out through the soles of your feet. Do this ten times and then forget about your breathing and let it go on naturally. The next step is to relax your body, piece by piece.

EXERCISE 2
Letting Go

Say to yourself, silently or whispered, "My left arm is feeling very heavy, my left arm is feeling heavy, my left arm is feeling very heavy." It will feel as though it were made of stone. Then continue, "My right arm is feeling very heavy, my right arm . . . " And so you continue to your left leg, your right leg, your neck and shoulders, and then on to your head and face. Gradually also create a sensation of warmth spreading all over your body in association with total relaxation. (If it is any easier, you may tape this autogenic exercise and let the tape guide you through this relaxation so you don't forget any part of your body.)

EXERCISE 3
Who Am I?

Now sit a while, relaxed, breathing easily, and just enjoy it. Begin by letting your mind wander, getting all those thoughts out of the way. Then begin to focus on yourself, using the questions we discussed earlier. By the way, your journal is on your lap, open and ready for some jottings.

Don't worry if you don't jot down anything. Maybe tomorrow or the next day, you will want to save a thought. You may also find it easier to write the questions at the top of a page in your journal as a reminder.

What happens to you? You might fall asleep. If you do, it may be because you are too tired to do the exercise, and you may want to change the appointed time. Or you may be trying to avoid finding out things about yourself. That's understandable, too. Don't worry. Keep trying, and eventually you will not fall asleep—in fact you'll have a good time thinking about yourself.

When you are finished with your half hour, you'll realize that you have discovered more positive things about yourself than negative ones. And it feels so good that you want to go out and do something nice for someone.

◊   ◊   ◊

When you first begin these exercises, you'll have difficulty concentrating on them. Don't worry. Remember, you didn't learn to ride a bicycle on the first try. But you persisted and eventually did ride one. So, persist and you will find you can concentrate and focus, and even better, someday you will be able to think of *nothing*, which is very restful!

Do these three exercises on a daily basis until you feel you have really gotten to know yourself. Dredge up some memories of the past—events of your childhood and even recent ones. You are the total of all your life experiences and the memories are stored in the memory bank of your right brain.[1] Your responses to your memories generate feelings, often negative feelings, which attach themselves to the memory of the experience. These feelings weigh upon you and repeat themselves whenever similar experi-

---

[1]To be discussed later in the book.

ences are confronted. Recognize the feelings when they surface, find some way to rationalize them and let them go. Everyone has memories that bring up feelings of pain, guilt, anger, resentment and jealousy. The memory itself need not be erased—in fact it is often pleasant to reminisce—but it would be more enjoyable if the memories did not dredge up unpleasant feelings. After the cleansing, your memories will be like reading the biography of someone else.

Later on in this chapter you'll learn an exercise for releasing and cleansing negative feelings from your memory. It is like brainwashing, except it's more positive for you are in control of the process, not some interrogator.

The exercise calls for activating your *mind-screen*. What is your mind-screen? It is like a television picture tube which sits between your eyes. It can be turned on at will. If you close your eyes and turn them upward, you can see it. Actually this is called the third eye, or the 6th chakra. When you want to use it, you turn on the power and it lights up like a TV. You are then able to program it with whatever images you wish. This is called visualization or guided imagery.

If you feel blocked, or think you can't "see" images, then try this test. Remember the last movie or play you saw? Recall a scene that made a great impression on you. *Imagine* it just as it took place, remembering the room or place, the people involved, and what they were saying and wearing. If you don't go to the movies, why not try recalling a familiar room in your home and recall all the objects on the walls and floor, beginning from the right of the entrance, traveling around until you end up to your left. If you are able to do either of these exercises, then you will have no problem visualizing. It's a tool that will be extremely helpful as you proceed to take charge of your life and become powerful.

Now let's get back to your mind-screen exercise. Program the screen to cleanse one of the negative feelings associated with a particular memory. Use anger, for instance. For example, maybe when you were young you had a brother who was smarter and better looking than you were, who was the favorite of the whole family. Every time your parents had to choose who would go on a trip, or who would get a pet dog, or have new clothes instead of hand-me-downs, it was always your brother who was chosen. You particularly remember the day your parents told all of you that there was only enough money to send one child to college and automatically everyone chose him. You felt deeply hurt at first, and then very angry and resentful toward the family. If this memory doesn't fit, dredge one up that you still feel angry about and use it for this exercise.

EXERCISE 4
Cleansing the Memory Bank

After you have chosen the memory to be cleansed, sit back in your special spot and do your breathing exercise with your eyes closed for ten minutes. With eyes still closed, turn up your eyes and switch on your mind-screen. Imagine picking up a special magic marker that lights up the screen wherever you draw a line, and begin to write the word ANGER. Carefully, one letter at a time, you write out the word in large letters. First, the A. Go over the letter with your pen once again before doing the N, and so on. When you have written the whole word, go over it once more to make sure that it's clear. Then study the word. Think about the meaning of anger, and the different kinds of anger there are, and different ways in which you and others express it. After a few minutes, the letters will slowly fade away until your screen is blank, but the power is still turned on.

Visualize your face in profile at the bottom right hand corner of the screen. Take a magic brush and paint a dot in the center of the screen using a color that you associate with anger. The color immediately spreads all over the screen and then is gradually replaced by the faces and events that caused your anger. Relive the time and feelings, linger awhile, and try to understand why these things did happen. As the picture begins to fade, you will be surprised that the feelings you associated with the events and people will also begin to lift and fade. You may wish to say something to the faces as they remain on the screen. Express the anger that you were unable to express at the time. Do so, it will help. Before ending the exercise, you may wish to bring forth more events and people associated with resentment and anger. Keep it up as long as it is not too uncomfortable for you. You may prefer to put it off for another day.

The exercise is not over yet. There is a need to remove the pain and residual anger from the memory. Turn off the power to your mind-screen, and, still with your eyes closed, turn them down toward your solar plexus, or energy center (the third chakra), and imagine a bright yellow light pouring out of it and spreading out completely around your body until you are a huge oval of golden yellow light. And then you'll feel healed and free of negative feelings as you return the cleansed memory to your memory bank.

◊   ◊   ◊

This exercise can be used for dealing with recent feelings or events as well as those in the far memory bank. Use it on a daily basis if you feel the need. Once you have learned the technique, you may use it during the day when you are driving or doing something that doesn't require much concentration. If you do it while driving, be assured that your reflexes are more attuned in the meditative state called Alpha than they would normally be. It is stress and the ensuing confusion which produce auto accidents.

So far nothing has been impossible to do. If you follow the exercises for a week, you will feel differently, a little more relaxed, less fatigued, and more hopeful than you have in a long time. You may decide to continue these mind-screen exercises for a while longer, which is perfectly all right, as you are the best judge of your needs.

2

Getting a Grip on Stress

Before we begin to take control of the stress in our lives, we need to understand the principle upon which our system of stress removal is based. There is an increasing interest in holistic medicine today. The concept has moved out of the arena of witchcraft, where it had been relegated by allopathic medical specialists, into daily life where it is more and more applied as a form of medical practice. Increasingly, doctors, psychiatrists, and other professionals are applying the holistic principle in their treatments.

In holistic theory we look at the human being as an integrated—or at least potentially integrated—unit. We consider the close relationship between mind, body and spirit when we consider the wellness or illness of a person. The concept is often illustrated as a triangle, for it represents the total person. (See figure 1 on page 10.)

It doesn't take a whole lot of discussion to prove the interrelationship between mind, body and spirit (or emotions, as some call the right side of the triangle). Psychosomatic illness is nothing new. For years we have known that a stomach ulcer is the product of emotional and mental stress, that headaches are symptoms of tension, or that lower back pain can be caused by tension, stress and even

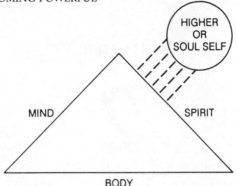

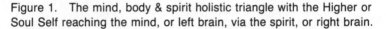

Figure 1. The mind, body & spirit holistic triangle with the Higher or Soul Self reaching the mind, or left brain, via the spirit, or right brain.

anger. Holistic practitioners accept this interrelationship and treat the *whole person* rather than just a symptom. This approach has worked when other systems have failed.

Holistic medicine is not new to the world, or to Westerners either, although we act as if we had just invented it. Traditional societies all over the world, including the American Indian society, have always treated mind, body and spirit simultaneously. The Indian shaman, the African witch doctor or the Sicilian herbalist has worked with this philosophy for hundreds of years. Not so many years ago holistic medicine was practiced in this country. What happened? Someone discovered the benefits of specialization. The priest or pastor was assigned the healing of the spirit, the psychologist or psychiatrist the healing of the mind, and the allopathic medical doctor the healing of the body. Seldom did they meet to discuss the patient. Imagine in the future how it will be when the professions join hands and work together to offer us health care once again.

If you take another look at the mind-body-spirit triangle and change the label of "mind" to left-brain, change "spirit" to right-brain and leave the "body" where it is, you may better understand what it means to take charge of your life—to become integrated. The higher self (or soul) sits free floating above the right-brain, which is why you can easily lose touch with it.

The primary functions of each side of the brain are listed in figure 2. It will become clear why certain things happen in your life that you feel you cannot control as you work with this list. When you are depressed, you have a feeling, and the feeling comes from the right-brain. But you don't know *why* you are depressed because the right-brain keeps it a secret. It keeps the secret because you are no longer integrated in the triangular sense; the triangle has been split up by an overload of stress which the body's natural healing system can no longer cope with. We will discuss the healing immune system later on in the section on healing. It is holistic in that it deals with all sides of the triangle simultaneously. When you feel a dis-ease, you are spread too thin and out of touch. You may even say, "I must get it together!" (You mean the triangle of course.)

An effective way to let depression go is to force yourself to do something with your hands that, within a short time, has a tangible or visible result. Clean and organize your hall closet, paint a picture, repair a broken lamp or polish the silver. By doing a job that requires creativity, spatial perception or imagination, you draw upon the energy that you have invested in depression to complete your task. What a surprise, as you admire the closet to discover that your depression has gone!

Good things come from the right-brain, too. When you paint a picture, invent a new sauce, or get a good hunch, you're using your right-brain. When you remember a name or event from the past, it comes from your memory bank in the right-brain. Recent memories stop temporarily in the left-brain but are eventually transferred.

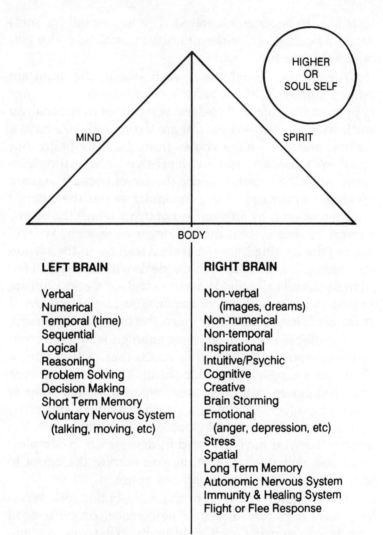

Figure 2. Activities associated with the left brain and right brain. The left brain is the rational, the right brain the intuitive and creative. When we are born we are right brain dominant, mixed dominant, or left brain dominant.

By the end of this handbook, you will have much better control over your right-brain and will be able to make it work more for you and less against you. The first step is to gain control of the stress that is coming to you from the right-brain. Since its source is the right-brain, you have to send the message back to the source to reduce the stress. Then you can feel more in charge of your life and *together* again.

If you look again at figure 2, you will see that the right-brain is non-verbal and uses imagery to communicate. Dreams are images, and their source is the right-brain. You must therefore use images to send your message to the right-brain if you want the stress reduced or lifted entirely. Visualizations or fantasies are your best means of communication. Although stresses sometimes take many years to build up, it is encouraging to know they can be reduced in *much less time*. So you can get rid of stress factors quickly when you learn how to do it.

Most people have been brought up to believe that the right-brain (or unconscious, as it was originally called) is a murky mischief-maker that is almost impossible to control; that the super ego (or censorship mechanism) kept control over the negative flow. This Freudian concept is still believed today. However, the right-brain (or unconscious) can actually be the most highly attuned component of your personality. It begins to cooperate once you send it the signal that you are going to take charge and use it as a tool in your growth.

Imagine having a good and close friend who, because of a lack of discipline and consistency, can be hurtful as well as helpful. You then demand of the friend certain concessions, a certain commitment and responsibility. It takes a while, but eventually the situation is under control. So you send the right-brain the message by assigning it, in the beginning, small tasks that have time limits. The right-brain doesn't like time: in fact, it doesn't truly understand it, since time was invented by the left-brain.

One of the tasks you assign the right-brain is to ask it at night, just before going to sleep, to remind you in the morning of the name and face of your third grade teacher. At first it might make you wait more than a day for the information, but eventually, as you give it more assignments, its responses will come faster. Give it problems that you are struggling with. Once you have assigned it the problem, you must forget about it consciously, otherwise it won't accept the assignment. It's as if you must give it an unconditional vote of confidence before it will undertake any assignment.

How often have you said, when trying to remember something, "I'll just forget it, and I know it will come to me in a few minutes." By forgetting it you are really saying to the right-brain that you trust it. Quite a different attitude from what most people have been taught.

Other ways of sending your right-brain requests for positive results is to send it images. Remember, it is reluctant to accept words as a means of communication and much prefers images. After all, it sends you messages through the images of dreams.

Stress

Now let's talk about stress. There are really two kinds of stress; one caused by the need to adjust to an external change of events, and the other—sometimes more difficult to deal with—caused by past feelings of guilt, resentment, anger, jealousy, emotional pain, etc. The exercises in chapter 1 are useful in eliminating these internal stresses. Both kinds are caused by our perceptions of our situations or ourselves.

What is stress? It is difficult to describe, as it is silent, invisible and unpredictable. In my workshops there have been several definitions of stress:

"Like a wind which blows all the time . . . "

"Like a constant invisible pressure . . . "

"Like living under water where everything is blurred"

"Like having someone looking over your shoulder all the time"

Some use the word *tension*, which is often a symptom of stress. You can be suffering from enormous degrees of stress and not even be aware of it. Most of you know when you feel stress and when you have more than you can handle.

When you are "together," and the sides of the mind, body, spirit triangle are joined, your natural healing system is able to cope with your stress and you are unaware of any difficulty. Everyone needs a certain amount of stress in order to function and survive. When the stress exceeds manageable limits, however, the triangle separates and health begins to deteriorate. It is interesting to note that for some reason the immune (or healing) system gives priority to dealing with emotional stress and neglects the body. The body takes anywhere from six months to two years to manifest the problem by breaking down with a serious disease, such as cancer, hypertension, heart trouble or other serious illnesses. Colds, allergies, asthma, or hay fever don't take as long to appear. Think back on the last cold you had; go back a few days before and remember the stressful situation which caused it.

Don't be reluctant to admit to yourself that the body frequently expresses emotional difficulties through illness. It's nothing to be ashamed of. And besides, the illness is just as real, whatever the source. What are the causes of external stress? Table 1 (on page 18) was devised by Drs. Thomas H. Holmes and Richard H. Rahe, psychiatrists at the University of Washington Medical School. Over the years since its creation, I have added a number of other changes that are more common today and make the list more helpful.

To use the table, check off the stress in the right hand column only if the *change* listed has happened in your life during the last twenty-four months. If you have experienced this change more than once, indicate in the space how many times it has happened—for example, mark it x2 for twice, and so on. Run a total on yourself. Add up all the numbers for changes that apply to you. Remember: the score you get is not etched in stone, and does not need to be taken too seriously. It is, however, an indication that you need to do some work on yourself. If your score is over 300, then you'd better go on reading this book! Chances are good—in our present day society—that you are approaching the three hundred mark, or even exceeding it. Most people who are still able to walk around seldom exceed a count of 950. Those with higher scores are not around; perhaps they are institutionalized.

I distribute a Personal Stress Assessment Form to participants in Stress and Life Management Weekends which I run from time to time. Make a list of the stresses in your life today. Also list those which might have accumulated in the last two years. Use the form shown in figure 3 on page 17 as a model. Take several sheets, head each sheet with a stress and then list the negative feelings you associate with it. When you have completed three or four

PERSONAL STRESS ASSESSMENT FORM

Indicate whether the stress is internal or external and give it a name.

STRESS:

_____

List below all the negative feelings, perceptions, situations or relationships that are associated with this stress.

SITUATIONS:

_____
_____
_____
_____

EVENTS:

_____
_____
_____
_____

NEGATIVE FEELINGS AND PERCEPTIONS:

_____
_____
_____
_____

Space below for additional comments.

_____
_____
_____
_____

Figure 3. A personal stress assessment form that can be used as a model and will be helpful in developing the chart in figure 4.

Table 1. Life Changes Ratings

Death of spouse	100	_____
Serious illness of spouse	80	_____
Divorce	73	_____
Marital separation	65	_____
Relationship breakup	63	_____
Jail sentence	63	_____
Death of a close family member	63	_____
Serious illness or accident in family	53	_____
Drug or alcohol addiction in family	52	_____
Marriage	50	_____
Fired from job	47	_____
Marital reconciliation	45	_____
Unemployed and looking for work	45	_____
Retirement	45	_____
Change in the health of family member	44	_____
Serious auto accident	43	_____
Death of a close friend	42	_____
Pregnancy	40	_____
Miscarriage	40	_____
Sexual problems	39	_____
Surgery	39	_____
Gain of new family member	39	_____
Business readjustment	39	_____
Change in income or financial status	38	_____
Change to different line of work	36	_____
Change in number of arguments with partner/spouse	35	_____
Mortgage over $20,000	31	_____
Victim of crime	30	_____
Foreclosure	30	_____
Change in responsibility at work	29	_____
Son or daughter leaving home	29	_____
Elderly parent moving home	29	_____

Table 1. continued

Troubles with in-laws	29	_____
Moving parent into nursing home	29	_____
Outstanding personal achievement	28	_____
Spouse begins or stops work	26	_____
Begin or end in school course	26	_____
Change in lifestyle	25	_____
Change in personal habits	24	_____
Trouble with boss	23	_____
Change in work hours or conditions	20	_____
Trouble with fellow worker(s)	20	_____
Change in residence	20	_____
Change in school	20	_____
Change in church activities	19	_____
Change in recreation	19	_____
Change in social activities	18	_____
Change in sleeping habits	16	_____
Change in eating habits (diet, vegetarian, etc.)	15	_____
Vacation	13	_____
Holiday	12	_____
Difficulties with bureaucracy	11	_____
Minor violations of the law	11	_____
Internal Stress Ratings*		
Unexpressed rage	95	_____
Chronic feelings of anger	80	_____
Chronic feelings of guilt	75	_____
Chronic feelings of fear	70	_____
Chronic feelings of pain	70	_____
Chronic feelings of failure and despair	65	_____

*Please include in your list if they apply.

sheets, prioritize them and save them for later when you create your own stress management program.

Symptoms of Unmanaged Stress

How do you know whether you have more stress than you can handle? Table 2 lists symptoms of excessive stress. Check the ones you can identify with.

As you identify with some of these symptoms, you may feel a sense of relief. At least you now know why these things are happening to you, and it's even more reassuring to know that others have the same problem.

In order to survive, most stressed people have devised various positive and negative techniques to deal with the surplus stress. You may already be doing some of the things found on the list in Table 3. Some of these techniques are excellent for temporarily reducing feelings of stress, but generally they deal only with the symptoms rather than the cause. In order to identify the cause, you

Table 2. Symptoms of Stress

Accidents and injuries	Indigestion
Buzzing in the ears	Insomnia
Cynicism	Rapid pulse and breath
Depression	Sexual problems
Disagreeableness	Shortness of breath
Excessive sleeping	Susceptible to germs
Fatigue	Swearing
Frequent colds	Turned-off feelings
Headaches (migraines)	Ulcers
High blood pressure	Unwillingness to plan
Hysteria	for future
Inability to concentrate	Vision problems

Table 3. Positive and Negative Techniques for Stress

Positive	Negative
Fantasy and daydreams	Alcoholism
Painting	Drug abuse
Music	Overeating
Dance	Anorexia nervosa, bulimia
Active sports	Gambling
Jogging	Risk-taking
Crying and giggling	Child and spouse abuse
Household pets	Sexual promiscuity
Hot baths, saunas, whirlpools	Frequent moves (house/job)
Prayer	Workaholism
Physical work (i.e., chopping wood)	Doctor hopping
Ceremony and ritual	Violence (crime)
Meditation	War
	Excess smoking (cigarettes or reefer)
	Radical causes
	Compulsive buying
	Avoiding reality
	Nervous or mental breakdown
	Calling in sick at work

have to do a personal inventory of your feelings, resentments, jealousies, pain and guilt, while at the same time carrying out the stress survey described earlier in this chapter.

If your total stress approached a score of three hundred, or was in excess of that figure, then on with it! It is difficult to be honest with yourself in carrying out an assessment. At times the right-brain will work very hard to block any insights that would help you in the process of dealing with stress. Don't accept the blocks as final; persist and eventually the right-brain will get the message and trickle out useful information. Remember to jot down in your journal all the information you receive, for you can use it later when you do your contemplative exercises using your mind-screen. Use patience when your right-brain blocks; impatience and anger exacerbate the blocks.

CHAPTER

3

Managing Stress in Your Life

In my work, I have found that in order to reach into the right-brain and either teach it or learn from it, it is necessary to reduce the activity of the left-brain to a minimum. This is accomplished through disciplinary exercises which do not require any particular skill. What the actual process is, specifically, I do not know, but it does work. It seems that the more disciplined the exercise of concentration, the more there is a gradual increase in the two-way flow between the two brains. Before the exercises, if the body and mind are very relaxed and tranquil, the right-brain is more receptive to being programmed or washed.

There are three steps which must be followed in order to reduce a particular stress; steps to be followed on daily basis. A daily half-hour seems to be the minimum required in order to accomplish the goal. We divide the half hour into three parts:

1) Ten minutes of physical relaxation through a numbered breathing exercise;

2) Five minutes of mental tranquilizing through visualization of a very peaceful scene;

3) Ten minutes of a visualization specifically designed to relieve a particular stress, and five minutes for winding down.

If you do the exercises faithfully on a daily basis, a subtle change will be noticeable after a week. In some cases, a very clear reduction of the stress had taken place. Continuing the exercise beyond the first week is sometimes indicated. If, at a later date, there seems to be a recurrence, then the particular visualization is repeated until the stress is again relieved. After working through the exercises in this handbook, you will be able to deal with whatever new stress appears or when old stress recurs in your life.

We now jump ahead to the most important step in your exercise program (phase three mentioned before), which is the creation of a visualization to deal with your number one stress. Let's label the stress "feelings of worthlessness." Take the stress assessment sheet where you listed all the negative feelings you associate with that particular stress, and study it carefully. Look at each feeling listed, separately, and think of the word which gives the opposite or positive feeling. Take, for example, the word "trapped." We often feel trapped in a stressful situation. The opposite is "free," isn't it? Another example might be the feeling of "inferiority." The opposite might be a "great accomplishment." The word "insecurity" might be turned into "trust," the word "fear" into "courage."

When you have found the opposites on your list of feelings, take a look at them and try to feel their effect upon you should they become a reality in your life. The next step is to pick a site or location for your visualization. Pick a spot anywhere in the world or universe. Remember, you hold a magic wand in your hand and can be anything—animal, human, or object—you can do anything in the world, anywhere. You might, for example, create the following visualization:

Over the years you have received a series of large foundation grants to support your research in a cure for hardening of the arteries and cholesterol build-up. You have discovered a peaceful tribe of people in Bali that have no history of heart trouble. You visit the tribe, who are fisher folk, and find them to be welcoming and peaceful people. As you begin your research, you realize that there is much work to be done here. So you build a beautiful home on the beach with a very modern laboratory building behind it. Your research moves ahead rapidly with frequent breakthroughs. Word has reached the medical world of your discoveries, and you have been awarded the Nobel Peace Prize. As you are reluctant to leave your laboratory and research for even a few weeks to receive the award in Sweden, the Award Committee has appointed a group of notable scientists to travel to Bali to make the presentation at your laboratory. You are also free to invite a group of friends and family to attend the ceremonies and following celebration. All their expenses will be borne by the Award Committee.

The special day has come! There is a great deal of activity in the cook house in the garden, as your servants prepare a feast of sea food, local fruits, and vegetables. Dozens of lobsters have been caught and are being kept alive and cool in the shade of the Banyan tree. You have chosen a Balinese silk sarong to wear and have put flowers in your hair, and as you walk out on the veranda, the seaplane bearing your guests is taxiing up to the beach. You walk down to greet them. Later, after several speeches, you receive the award. You then lead your guests to the long, food-laden table in the garden and urge them to enjoy themselves. Musicians, hidden behind the trees, play softly on local flutes and stringed instruments.

After the banquet in the garden, you bid your guests goodnight as they make their way to the guest houses along the beach, and you walk down to the water's edge, enjoying the reflection of the moon on the waves, and the gentle sliding sound the waves make as they retreat. You turn and amble toward your villa, looking forward to a good night's sleep.

You are now ready to go to work on the stress we call "feelings of worthlessness" using this visualization in the last ten minutes of your half hour meditation. The relaxation and visualizations must be done in silence, unless you want to whisper to yourself from time to time. The use of champagne bubbly, or waterfall music on tapes or records, is not recommended. They make our brain lazy and euphoric and give it a false sense of well-being. If you listen to these tapes or records, use them while you are doing a boring job, driving in traffic or trying to get to sleep, but not while you are meditating.

EXERCISE 5

Alpha One

Let everyone in the house know that you are not to be disturbed for half an hour. Move to your special spot and begin your exercise. Sit comfortably, close your eyes and begin by expelling all the air from your lungs forcefully, so you make a wheezing sound. Now begin by breathing in slowly, from the diaphragm through your nostrils to the count of eight. When you exhale, suck in your stomach, and then begin your inhalation by pushing out your stomach, and then fill the upper lungs. Hold your breath and count silently to four. Then exhale slowly to the count of eight. Immediately inhale again to the count of eight and follow the same pattern. There are several reasons for holding your breath to the count of four: (1) to prevent hyperventilation, and (2) to benefit from the greatest moment of healing when you are concentrating on holding your breath. The Indian yogis who developed this style of numbered breathing discovered that the holding of the breath was extremely beneficial in reestablishing the natural balance of mind, body, and spirit.

Continue counting with your eyes closed for at least five minutes and then test yourself. You should feel extremely relaxed physically. You may have a sense of being in harmony with all your parts and surroundings, as well. Test yourself by stopping the counted breathing, and take a little breath and then hold your breath for several seconds before repeating another little shallow breath. If this seems comfortable to you, then continue in this way for another two minutes and then forget entirely about your breathing and let it happen unconsciously.

If, on the other hand, you tense up, return to the numbered breathing for a few more minutes, and then test yourself again. When you first begin these daily exercises, you may find it very difficult to totally relax and enjoy them. Persist, and every day they will become easier and more enjoyable. The secret is to persist while at the same time accepting any temporary failure. Do the best you can. It is not advisable to force yourself to relax; it is self-defeating.

EXERCISE 6

Inner Tranquility

Now that the first ten minutes are over, it is time to visualize a very peaceful place where you are all alone while feeling a very deep mental tranquility. You have left all your cares and worries somewhere behind you, and you enjoy the feeling of an uncluttered mind. The spot you pick might be a tropical beach, a moss-covered bank of a stream, a silent ride in a hot-air balloon skimming over dew-covered fields; or you might be sitting in the shade of a giant tree with your back pressed against its cool trunk, or soaring up in the sky using your creamy white feathered wings to catch the thermals.

Really get involved in the scene you have chosen, enjoy the stillness, the aloneness, the slow movement of the waves, clouds, or stream. Feel as though you have become what you are watching.

When you have achieved the mental tranquility, a strange — and sometimes slightly frightening — feeling will come over you. Don't be frightened. Remember, as long as you do not use any artificial means or chemicals to achieve this high, you are perfectly safe and always in control. It will seem as if you have turned into cool marble, and that the whole environment is holding its breath. You may also feel that you are falling gently, without fear, knowing that you will not hurt yourself. Enjoy this sensation; it is probably the first time you have been truly tranquil and relaxed in many years. Enjoy this sense of peace and tranquility for about ten minutes and then move into the visualization that deals with your specific stress. Get into it in great detail, and take your time to enjoy every experience as it comes. Do not worry whether or not your half hour is up. It probably isn't. Visualizations are like dreams; they seem to take a great deal of time, but they don't actually. Remember how often you have awakened in the morning in the middle of a dream, and how you pushed the snooze button on the alarm, and got back into your dream or another one just as complicated? You woke in a panic, believing that you were very late and did not hear the second alarm, and to your surprise only a minute or two had passed. As I mentioned earlier, time is a creation of the left-brain and is not needed by the right-brain, which gives you dreams. We used to hear that people who are in the process of drowning, which certainly doesn't take but a few minutes, pass their whole life in review during those few minutes. Here the right-brain memory bank is at work, not needing the structure of time.

When your time is up, gradually open your eyes, straighten up and blink a few times before you rise to leave your spot. Move slowly at first.

After some practice, you'll be reluctant to leave your visualization. It feels so good and becomes so real that it is difficult to face mundane life-issues again. But you are in better shape to deal with the issues than you were when you began your meditation. On certain days when you anticipate some unexpecteds, indulge yourself in a few extra minutes to be better prepared.

◊ ◊ ◊

In the life management groups that I run, I use a slightly different method for identifying and picturing feelings associated with stress. The group also writes the visualization down on a chart. For the chart, you can use a large piece of newsprint and a blue magic marker. (I emphasize blue rather than black, because it has a positive effect on the viewer.) On the upper left hand half of the sheet, I draw an outline of a tree in full leaf, and I label the tree with whatever stress we wish to work on. The tree has no root system until we begin to draw one, one root at a time. Each root is labeled with a negative feeling associated with the stress. When you have exhausted your search for feelings, you'll find that you have a very complicated root system. This process is extremely helpful, as it forces you to analyze stress from the right-brain perspective. It gives everyone in my workshops a much deeper understanding of the problem. (See figure 4 on page 32.)

The next step is to create a visualization for meditation. Every effort is made to recognize the positive opposites of the "roots" and incorporate them in the visualization which is written in clear letters in a squared-off section of the right hand side of the chart.

It is important that this stress chart be hung somewhere in your home (or workplace) and looked at frequently. During the day, as you pass, give it a glance. It is not necessary to stop and stare and read it. A brief glance offers a visual reminder to the right-brain, the source of stress, that it has been involved in developing the chart, and now has the task of relieving the stress which is of its own making. The right-brain begins to get the message, and during the meditation it will be much more cooperative.

Participants soon learn to develop their own stress charts in order to respond to newly discovered stresses in their lives, and you may want to use this idea.

◊   ◊   ◊

At the end of the first week of dealing with a specific stress using the visualization for it, you must decide whether to continue with it or create a new one for another stress. Few stresses, particularly ones which are high on the priority list, can be dealt with successfully in one week. Continued use is recommended. However, if you are becoming bored, put the visualization aside for a week and return to it later. Create a new visualization for the number two stress. Although your list of stresses may seem long initially, you will find that as soon as you have reduced the first three or four, the others seem to evaporate. That's because you have reduced the amount of stress to a level where your natural healing mechanism (or immune system) can take over. When this moment arrives, you'll recognize it easily because you'll feel great relief and unexplained happiness.

The following visualizations have been used by participants in my Stress Management Workshops. You may find them helpful. First we will discuss a problem that needed to be overcome. Then we work with a special visualization to cure the problem. The results of the visualization are also discussed because these solutions and results may help you to formulate some of your own visualizations geared to solve your own special kinds of stress.

PROBLEM 1

Stress on the Job

A highly trained technician worked at a naturally stressful job running a circuit console at a regional electric power company. He enjoyed the challenge and the responsibility which his job demanded. He got along well enough with his colleagues, but his boss was driving him crazy. The boss, a non-technical administrator, and an efficient one at that, clearly felt some inadequacy in not understanding the intricate operation of the sophisticated circuit console. During circuit blowouts, usually caused by lightning or nesting squirrels, the technician had to fully concentrate in

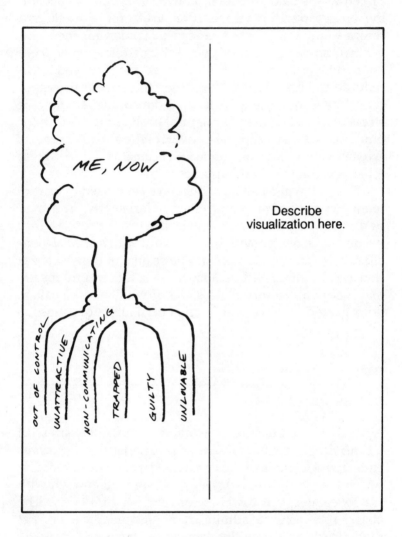

Figure 4. An example of a personal stress chart. Use at least an 8½ by 11 inch sheet of paper. This might be the way someone would "draw" low self-esteem.

order to avoid a regional blackout. It seemed that whenever an emergency hit, his boss rushed to the control room and hovered over him asking stupid questions.

Visualization

The participant visualized a farewell party for his boss which was to celebrate his transfer and promotion to a regional office where he would have training responsibilities in local offices. The atmosphere was cheerful and congratulatory.

Result

A few months later the boss was contacted by high level executives in the company and asked if he would undertake to design a training program for control room personnel. His responsibilities would include frequent absences from his office, and his old supervisory responsibilities would be shared between the technician and his friend and colleague. The technician was later offered a college training program which would assure him later promotions by the company.

PROBLEM 2

Stress at Home

A woman participant had a teen-age son whose negative attitude around the home was very stressful for her. He hardly spoke to his father, accepted punishment by sulking and being grouchy, and made no effort to carry his load in household chores. When asked to cut the lawn, or do any other household duties, his immediate response was to ask how much money he would be paid. She was particularly worried about a confrontation between father and son as her husband had suffered a heart attack the year before.

Visualization

It is late Saturday morning on a summer day. The sound of the lawn mower has just ended, and as she looks out the kitchen window, she sees her son and his father gathering up the gardening tools to take to the garage. They come into the kitchen and announce they are going to the lake for an afternoon of fishing. They rummage together in the refrigerator and pull out sandwich makings. With a lot of kidding and laughter, they create two "dagwoods" which they have difficulty jamming into sandwich bags. They absentmindedly kiss her and rush out to the garage to load their fishing gear. The sound of the engine starting and the car backing out of the driveway bring a smile to her face.

Result

Within two weeks the participant began to see subtle changes in her son's and husband's responses to each other. Soon, she was sure, they would begin to communicate again.

PROBLEM 3
No Time for Yourself!

A wife and mother who worked the night shift in a terminal ward of a local hospital felt increasingly that she was all those things but she was no longer a person, nor did she ever have an opportunity to do something for herself. One morning she had to straighten up the kitchen and the house, do the laundry, clean out her husband's closet and take his winter suits to the cleaners, buy a birthday gift for her mother-in-law, pick up her son at school and drive him to football practice, arrange for her daughter's ballet lessons, plan and cook the dinner and find time to rest before her husband came home from work. Just thinking of her schedule for the day, and the schedule of her life, made her feel angry and then guilty. She knew that in order to survive, she had to take some immediate steps.

Visualization

It is a winter evening and the scene is her kitchen. The windows are steamy from cooking. The family has finished its favorite dinner of spaghetti and meatballs, and the two children, having volunteered to do the dishes, are finishing up at the sink. She and her husband are sitting watching them work. They come over and ask, "What next, Mom?" She tells them to sit at the empty table, for the family is going to play a very important game— important for her survival and the family's welfare.

She picks up a market bag and dumps the contents in the center of the table. There lies a pile of cardboard cubes, and each cube had words written on it: "Ballet lessons," "Oil change and grease job," "Football practice," "Birthday card for the teacher," "Dry cleaners," and so on. She tells her husband and children that the game is to study each cube very carefully to decide if it is important to the family's survival. If not, the cube is to be thrown back in the bag.

Cube by cube, they slowly eliminate the pile until only three cubes remain. After a lot of serious discussion, the family decides that these three are essential to the survival of the family. On the cubes are written the following words: "Love," "Good Health," and "Good Communication."

Result

After using the visualization in her meditation for one week, the participant could begin to see a difference in her attitudes and a reduction in her headaches. She could see that she was making better use of her time and discovering periods during the day that she could devote to herself exclusively. Her husband and children were delighted by her cheerfulness and apparently more positive attitude. In a few weeks she began to plan on dealing with the next stress on her list.

4

Making Visualization Work for You

In chapter 1, we talked about using the mind-screen to cleanse negative feelings from your memories. As you continue to work on these feelings, you will soon find that it's very easy for you to turn on your mind-screen. There are other ways you can use your mind-screen that can positively affect your future.

Holding an image on your mind-screen will not only affect your internal environment, but also your external environment. Remember when you were a child you used to throw pebbles in pools or ponds and watch the rings spread? As long as there was a water surface, they would reach the shore and make the grass wave, or frogs jump, or even move pebbles and debris at the water's edge. When you begin the process of integrating your two brains and developing spiritually, you drop a pebble in your environment. Very soon after you begin the exercises, your friends and family will take note of changes taking place in you. They will find themselves changing, too, for they will adjust to your development. We do not live in a world of our own, insulated from others; this is why other people's negativity often threatens positive feelings you have. There is a constant interchange of feelings and energy and thoughts between you and all those with whom you come in contact. If you send positive thoughts in the direction of someone who wallows in negativity, you either help them to come out of the negativity, or you threaten his or her way of life, and he or she fights back.

There was an interesting article in *Psychology Today* (July 1982) entitled "Self-fulfilling Stereotypes." It mentions a very interesting experiment which was carried out by Professor Albert King at Northern Illinois University. Professor King had a theory that he wanted to test; that perceptions we have of people can change them. He located a trade school and contacted the welding instructor. He had chosen at random from the enrollees the names of five who he identified for the instructor. He told him that they had been found to have an unusually high aptitude for the coursework. The enrollees were not informed of this report and the instructor was urged not to share the information with them. During the course, the five showed in their performance the effect of the instructor's perceptions. They were absent less often than the other workers, learned the trade in half the time than the others required, and scored ten points higher on their final welders' test. Finally, the other trainees chose them as the five preferred workers of the whole group.

What is particularly significant here is that the students were not aware of their designation. The instructor, alone, by projecting their performance, could affect it.

There are times when everyone looks forward to a meeting or event in the future with dread or a fear of failing. If you continue to hold on to these feelings right up until the meeting or event, you can be sure it will be dreadful, and you will not accomplish your goals. On the other hand, if you visualize the meeting or event with confidence and hopefulness, you will project that feeling onto others who are involved, and they will feel compelled to fulfill your expectations. The power of positive thinking, which most of you have heard about all your life, works on the same principle. The kind of energy generated when you are feeling positive feels so good to others that they respond in a positive way. Those who cannot respond this way have structured their lives on negativity and are threatened by the energy of positive thinking. They require a great deal of patience. It's difficult to give up the negativity you know for the positive unknown. It's like giving up a pair of old shoes that have no more arch and tend to leak in puddles. The new pair might improve your walk and posture but they also might pinch at first.

It will be helpful at this stage to try creative visualization and learn how it can work for you in many, many ways. A modest beginning with good results will encourage you to expand your uses of it.

EXERCISE 7
Granted Favors

Go to your special spot and sit quietly. Think of a meeting or event in the near future, and decide how you wish it to conclude. Perhaps you are going to ask a special favor of someone and you want them to grant it. Your visualization will be of *the favor having been granted*. See yourself thanking the person and enjoying the results. It is vital that you believe in your capacity to accomplish your goal. Trust in the method and it will produce. Remember how we discussed using the right-brain to remember things or solve problems, and how important it was to have confidence in its capacity?

After breathing slowly and deeply, with your eyes closed, look up to your mind-screen and see your goal as having been accomplished. Watch yourself and others discussing the accomplishment and its effects on you. You might hug or shake the hand of the person. Work on this visualization until it is clear on your mind-screen, and then reduce it to its essentials. Reduce it to a still photo of the results or accomplishment.

When you have reduced the event, repeat silently to yourself that you know your goal will be reached; that you have full confidence in the method as it has worked in the past for you and for many others who use it. That is the end of the exercise.

However, during the day, when you have a brief moment to yourself, repeat the image on your mind-screen, and affirm its success, just as you did at home. You will find that after a while the visualization automatically appears at various times during the day. The more it does, the easier it will be to accomplish your goal.

There are many ways to use visualization in your life. It is important to use the techniques only for positive gain and not at the sacrifice of someone else's happiness or well-being. Used destructively, it boomerangs and becomes self-destructive. Upon discovering the power of visualization, some people are tempted to use it to manipulate, to get even, and in some instances, to make a person ill. This then becomes black magic and is a dangerous game to play.

This method of visualization works well in the area of emotional pleasures, love and fulfillment. It is very effective for relationships. Let's say you are having difficulty with a fellow worker or a member of your family. What are the steps to improve your relationship? Search for the positive qualities and talents in the other person. (Everyone has them.) Visualize your benefiting and enjoying the product of these qualities and talents. Feel excited and grateful, as if you just made a wonderful discovery. Hold that vision for a few days and you will notice an entirely new response pattern developing in that person. Why? When you change your internal environment, the external environment responds and adjusts to you.

Set goals for yourself and hold the vision that your goal has been accomplished. Good health, a new career, beauty, prosperity, inner peace, success for a loved one, improvement in your game, finding just the right place to live, receiving an invitation from someone you would like to know better, and so forth. The goals you set are realized when you meet the following conditions:

1) Believe in and trust the method.

2) Wish for something that will not harm anyone or be against another's will.

3) Create a clear picture of your goal as accomplished; don't dwell on the *process* of achieving it.

4) Recall the picture frequently during the day, and particularly at night (just before going to sleep), and in the morning when you awake. You are more in touch with your right-brain at these times. Add a silent affirmation that you are confident your goals will be achieved.

5) For the first exercises, set no time limits and make the goals small. Later, with growing confidence, you may become more ambitious. It is not a question of whether the system works, but rather how skillful you become making it work.

◇　　　◇　　　◇

At times, after working on a visualization for a few days, you may find you no longer want it to happen as you set it. Acknowledge your change of mind, adjust the visualization accordingly, or abandon it completely. Be grateful you discovered this before the goal became a reality. This is a very good way to separate the "real needs" from the "maybe wants."

CHAPTER

5

Using Your Spirit Guide

As you develop and make use of your right-brain skills, you'll make some discoveries which will greatly help you manage your daily life. One of these is the valuable support and advice you receive from your spirit guide, or Higher Self.

In the past, during periods of confusion as to what to do next, or how to understand a situation, you may have felt you had an invisible self which intervened and helped you see things more clearly. It might have seemed as if you had a silent partner and good friend always around. Until now, you may not have learned to summon your spirit guide quickly when you need its advice. This chapter, with its visualization exercise, will greatly help in establishing a more reliable relationship with your guide.

Who is your spirit guide? A soul in orbit around you? A dead ancestor? Some theorize that it is your right-brain. It is difficult to believe that it is part of your right-brain; however, it sits above it, as shown in figure 2 on page 12. When it "talks" to you, it often comes up with entirely opposite responses than you would anticipate. And it's amazing, but it's always right! Its advice is always the best, sometimes better than the advice of a good friend.

This is probably because your spirit guide does not have an ego at stake when it gives advice, and it really knows your needs.

Before you can really use your spirit guide, you have to learn to listen to it. And before you can really "hear" it you need to relax your body and still your mind, just as you do in the stress management exercises. In addition, you will have to create an image of it in order to recognize it. Your guide will appear in your visualizations or in your dreams from time to time.

In your visualization you will now create a private sanctuary where you will always meet your spirit guide. This sanctuary must be really private and secure. Usually the sanctuary that most people choose is outdoors and scenic, but it does not necessarily have to be. You might be more at peace and secure in a round room in a tower, or in the nave of a church, or in a secret place under the front porch. Before you begin the next exercise, decide where you wish to meet your spirit guide. During the exercise you will arrange to meet there every time you wish a consultation in the future. You may discover, as happens often, that your spirit guide will not say anything at your first meeting. You may even have difficulty describing the guide after your first exercise is over, even though you were well aware of a presence in your private sanctuary. The secret is to be patient and confident that at one of your next meetings a conversation will begin. Very often people summon the guide out of curiosity more than need. You may already have the answer to the question you are going to ask. In that case, your guide will not appear. For our first meeting, preparations will have to be more elaborate than for later ones. In fact, you will get so good at arranging meetings that just by closing your eyes briefly, your spirit guide will appear and answer you.

EXERCISE 8
Meeting Your Spirit Guide

Go to your special spot and sit in a comfortable position. Close your eyes, expel the air from your lower lungs force-fully, and begin your numbered breathing pattern of eight/four/eight. Follow the exercise just as you did in chapter three. This time, instead of dealing with a particular stress through visualization, substitute going to your private sanctuary, settling in, becoming comfortable, and waiting patiently for the arrival of your guide. If your sanctuary is outdoors, you can visualize your guide as a speck on the horizon slowly approaching until it becomes either a person, animal, or even ball of light or color. If you are indoors, then perhaps a very gentle knocking on a door, and a very gradual opening of the door will reveal your spirit guide. When your guide approaches, offer the seat next to you and give your guide time to get used to you before you speak. You may just look at one another for awhile. You will want to confirm that it is the one for whom you are waiting. Ask it silently whether it is your real spirit guide. If the answer is affirmative, you will want to arrange a method for meeting in the future. Ask if there is any special way or signal required. If you do not have any pressing problems to be solved, or questions to be asked, the spirit guide will probably rise and bid you goodbye and slowly go away. Your feelings at the end of the exercise will include a deep sense of gratitude and relief. And excitement, of course! You have just identified and established contact with the best friend you will ever have.

CHAPTER

6

Developing Your Psychic Tools

You all have inherent psychic abilities and skills whether you develop them or not. If you *do* begin the process of opening and development, it is absolutely essential that you approach it with reverence and a degree of humility. Reverence and humility do not negate having fun or a sense of humor, but they clearly define the enormous responsibility that goes along with the process. With psychic skills developed, you are able to help other people blossom into joyful spirituality or mislead them through the pains and feats of darkness and hell. It is almost as if you have been given a magic wand that can do anything, and it is up to you to decide how to use it.

The awakening of your abilities is very exciting and you will want to tell someone about it. Choose a good friend or relative, and share your progress with someone. Your friend may not be able to understand and might ridicule you. Accept that as inevitable, and visualize or fantasize making a new friend who will understand. That friend will materialize.

As you work along with these exercises, you will gradually become aware of an increase in hunches, unexplained feelings, dreams with clear messages, deja vu experiences, and possible visions into the future. Do not be frightened by these, but accept them prayerfully, knowing that when the time is right, you will be told what to do with them.

People have been referred to me by psychiatrists and therapists for training in controlling psychic experiences that were disrupting their lives and causing them and their families unnecessary anguish. Sometimes in one two-hour session, or over a period of several weeks, they have been able to take control. A simple visualization is to imagine a toggle switch in the right-brain which can easily be flipped off and on. This switching ability will increase in efficiency as you work with the following exercises.

After taking control, inevitably you'll look for a creative and constructive way to use your skills. Many people turn to healing as a natural next step. First you need to heal yourself and maintain a high degree of wellness. Then you can turn to help families and friends. Later, you may find an organization needing volunteers to make home or hospital visitations. The outlets for this energy are myriad.

Before proceeding with the exercises ask yourself the following questions. Honest answers are vital to your own spiritual growth.

1) Am I free of internal stresses due to old feelings of pain, resentment, guilt and jealousy?

2) Have I forgiven myself for the pain I have caused and forgiven those who have caused me pain?

3) Have I reduced my external stresses to the point where I feel daily periods of true inner peace?

If the answers are affirmative, then proceed with this chapter and you will be able to achieve your goals. If you answer no to these questions, then do some more work with your mind-screen, and on your internal and external stresses. There is no reason to build expectations unless you have a reasonable chance of realizing them.

The exercises that follow can be done in your daily half-hour period. If you wish to accelerate the process, do two or three exercises at a time, or take a two-hour period on the weekend and do a group of them. They are great fun to do! If you feel the strain of concentration is about to give you a headache, then stop for a while and walk around, or do something that needs doing. These exercises are never painful or uncomfortable.

At this stage of your development, additional equipment is required: a hand-wound timer, an inexpensive portable cassette player/recorder and some half-hour tapes.

I will list the exercises in the order that you are to do them. However, it does not in any way interfere with your learning if you decide to repeat them. If your feeling is that you should, then accept the message from your right-brain. You are now able to listen to your hunches and follow them with more confidence. They are always right until you judge or modify them with the logical left-brain. Leave them pure and they will be the truth.

Before you do any of these exercises, use exercise 1 on page 2, "Energizing Breath."

EXERCISE 9

Opening the Channel

Set your minute timer for five minutes. Sit in your spot and begin breathing in, and as you do, feel the energy beginning at your feet and working its way up to your head. When you exhale, release all the unpleasant feelings and things which have happened to you since the last meditation.

EXERCISE 10
Focusing

Set your timer again for five minutes. Now turn your eyes up to your mind-screen and visualize the following:

> You are sitting in a circle of warm white sand in a meditative position. On the outer edge of the circle are many friendly but undisciplined thoughts that look like brown amoeba blobs. It is essential that you keep them from moving closer onto your white sand. You find that from time to time one will begin to crawl toward you, like a child, to be closer to you. You see yourself firmly pushing it back with your hand until it is beyond the limit of your sand. Fortunately you also have eyes in the back of your head. You see one in back trying to sneak onto your sand. You turn and with love and firmness you force it back. This goes on for a few minutes but you soon see a change. These thoughts which interfere with your concentration are finally beginning to get the message and they no longer try to enter your circle of white sand.

You are now ready to concentrate on the exercises which follow. Use these first two exercises at the beginning of every session. Record on your tape what your feelings were, and how successful you felt the exercise was.

EXERCISE 11
Take a Trip

Now set your timer for ten minutes. Place a grapefruit, orange, or apple in front of you on a piece of white cloth or on a paper napkin. You may do this exercise with your eyes open all the time, or closed most of the time, whichever is easier for you. Imagine that you are taking a trip into the fruit, and that the first step is either to grow smaller or make the fruit much bigger. Do that and then figure how you are going to get into it without damaging it. Enter it. Feel, smell, taste, and see all its qualities. Sample all its parts and see yourself moving freely from one part to the other. Take your time, as there are many details not to be missed. You may have visions, or even meet people on this trip, but it is essential to know what it's like to be the fruit. When the timer rings, leave the fruit quietly and see yourself moving back to where you are sitting. You will regret having to leave the fruit.

Record a thorough description of all the sensations and events of the trip on your tape.

If you are doing these exercises in your half-hour periods, this is probably all you can do for now. In the evening you might find it useful to listen to the tape. Keep the tape as a record of your progress.

EXERCISE 12
Sea Sounds

Set your timer for ten minutes. Begin with exercises 9 and 10 to prepare yourself. If you own a large, snail-like seashell, or a glove, place it before you. Again, as with the fruit, you are going on a trip. This time you'll be in the seashell or in the glove. Every corner is to be explored, and all sensations, colors, and feelings are to be enjoyed. If you have found a turban shell or conch shell, travel to the very tip and find out what is there. Feel the texture against your bare skin, and remember the smells and sound effects. When the timer rings, leave the shell or glove, and quietly come back to external reality.

Record on your tape a thorough description of all your sensations and thoughts while you were taking the trip.

EXERCISE 13
Controlled Blinking

Set your timer for five minutes. Begin with your usual preparatory exercises. Throw a coin on the floor, or pick a tiny spot on the wall and concentrate on it. This exercise is to be done with your eyes open, unless they need a brief rest. The purpose here is to learn to totally focus on a dot or small object, and to try to keep your eyes from blinking. Obviously you will have to blink eventually, but try not to for as long as you can stand it. Without any lubrication your eyes may begin to burn. Never mind, as the tears which come will lubricate them. After a while you will find that all your concentration is focused on keeping your eye on the point and not blinking. All other thoughts are pushed aside. When the timer rings, allow yourself to shut your eyes for a few minutes to rest them. There is no need for recording your impressions, unless you wish to keep a record.

EXERCISE 14
Imposing on the Right Brain

This exercise is progressive in that it commands the right-brain to perform. You are going to raise and lower your skin temperature. When you get really good at this one, you can use it to raise a fever in your body (or in a particular area) for self-healing. We will discuss this later.

Set your timer for ten minutes. Begin with exercises 9 and 10 to prepare yourself. Imagine that you are being slowly lowered into a tank of warm water. The water temperature is a few degrees higher than your normal body temperature. First your toes feel the warmth, and then, gradually, very gradually, the level of warm water rises up your legs, up your torso and arms, until it reaches the top of your head. Since you are holding a snorkel in your mouth, you are able to breathe easily. The surface of your skin will feel much warmer than normal as your capillaries dilate. Your skin almost feels as if you had a fever. Your head feels particularly hot, and your forehead may actually sweat a bit.

After a few minutes, feel yourself being slowly lifted out of the warm water, and as your skin becomes exposed to the air it feels abnormally cold. When the water level gets below your shoulders, you will shiver and feel the chill on your back. When your toes leave the water, you feel uncomfortably cold everywhere. Hold the cold sensation for only a minute or two more, and begin gradually to restore your natural body temperature until you feel comfortable again. Enjoy normal body temperature until the timer bell rings.

EXERCISE 15

Giant to Dwarf

Set your timer for ten minutes. Again, prepare with exercises 9 and 10. This exercise is done to create the feeling of being very small and very large. Imagine yourself in a room that you know well. As you watch, you see yourself becoming very small. You feel your skin shrinking, your mouth becoming small, your arms and legs shortening, your face shrinking and your ears becoming tiny. Decide then how small you are willing to become. Aim for being five inches tall, for example, and when you are, stop reducing in size. Now look up and around you, and notice how different things look from this angle. The next step is to grow abnormally large. Feel your body expanding, legs and arms becoming very long, your head expanding, almost as if it were being blown up like a balloon. You decide that you cannot become any taller than the ceiling. When your head brushes the ceiling, you stop growing and begin to look around. Everything looks too small to you. You also see dust on the top edges of things that is not visible when you are normal size. You are afraid to move for fear that you might break some object. When the timer bell rings, reduce your size to what you normally are, and slowly open your eyes.

Record on tape a thorough description of what your feelings were as you changed size. Any other observations should be recorded as well.

7

Life Energy and Thought Forms

Before beginning the next phase of developing your psychic skills, you need to understand the meaning of the life force. Later on in this chapter you will also need to know the meaning of thought forms.

It is not difficult to tell when your energy level is low. Most people talk about it frequently, but take the words for granted, without knowing its source or what it is really. It is as much a mystery as electricity, and similar in many ways. Its source is the sun. Everything that the sun touches becomes energized—people, trees, stones, plants, vegetables, grain, animals, and all inanimate objects. This energy is transmitted either directly—as when you feel the sun's warmth on your skin—or indirectly—when you eat vegetables, grain, or meat. Without the sun's energy, life as it is known to us would be non-existent.

Have you noticed how in winter, when the sun (in the northern hemisphere) is its farthest from you, you feel very low on energy? When your energy level reaches a certain low, you feel depressed, exhausted, unable to cope—almost as if your life were snuffing out. February has the highest suicide rate in the north. Ever wonder why? Because after several months of low energy intake, for some suicide seems the only way out. Why do people go to the Caribbean or south in the winter, and why is February the peak of the season there? In the fall as the sun's energy reduces, leaves fall off the trees, the sap runs into the ground, plants die, and animals hibernate. Unfortunately, among humans only yogis have learned the techniques of hibernation. We have learned to produce electricity which can be made to partially supplement some of the sun's energy. Ultra-violet, ultra-red, mercury lamps, or grow-lights are all sun substitutes. If plants are given a sixteen-hour daily dose of broad spectrum light during the winter, they grow and produce flowers, seeds and fruit.

We all give off energy, particularly when we are in good health. We tend to store the energy in our bodies for future use. The surplus radiates in visible and invisible energy fields. The visible field is called an aura. We will begin to see both before we finish this book. The polar energy, Aurora Borealis, very closely resembles the aura which radiates from a person, animal, tree, plant, stone, or object, although the latter is much less obvious to the naked eye. To achieve the ultimate goal of "seeing" both the invisible and visible aura, you have to pass through several stages of cognition or seeing.

As you are now beginning to reach into the right brain and consciously use its intuitive or psychic skills, the preparation for the exercises is lengthy and requires more effort. You must reach a very deep level of meditation, which will require most of your half hour. The first preparatory exercise will use your mind-screen, once you feel you are fully relaxed and mentally tranquil.

◊   ◊   ◊

EXERCISE 16

Integration

Set your timer for twenty-five minutes. You will be combining three exercises in this one. Go to your spot and sit comfortably, and begin your preparatory exercise for a few minutes. Next use exercise 2, "Letting Go," on page 3, which begins: "My left arm feels heavy, my left arm feels very heavy, my left arm . . . " When you are finished with all the parts of your body, move on to your most peaceful place as indicated in exercise 6, "Inner Tranquility" (see page 28), and feel comfortably alone, secure and at peace. Enjoy this place for a time, savoring all its qualities of sound, vision, feel, and texture.

Now slowly turn your closed eyes up to your mind-screen and imagine the following scene: You see two hands; the one on the left is yellow and has its open palm turned upward as if to receive a gift. This represents your left brain or conscious mind. The hand on the right is a pale blue, and has a closed fist turned downward. This hand represents the right brain, which is about to share its skills with you by releasing its secrets from its closed fingers. As you watch, the two hands come together, the yellow left hand slowly sliding in under the blue right hand, and the blue right hand moving to meet it half way. The hands stop moving, and the poised right hand begins to open very slowly, one finger at a time. You feel an excitement that is difficult to explain, but as the fingers open, you feel a kind of energy spreading throughout your body. It is not frightening, but gives you a feeling of trust and security, as if an old friend had come back into your life again. When the two hands are fully opened, they begin to fade, and you know you are now ready to accept your psychic skills with reverence and love. Sit, enjoying this feeling until the timer rings.

◊   ◊   ◊

To prepare for seeing visible energy fields and auras, you will have to gather a few objects to study. Choose objects that are old, or well-used and handled. Select a house plant which seems to be very healthy. Bring all the objects to your spot, but use only one at a time. If you have a piece of plain dark cloth, place it over the seat and back of a wooden straight-backed chair and face it toward you.

EXERCISE 17
First Look at Energy Fields

Set your timer for ten minutes. Assuming that you have already gone through the preparatory exercises 9 and 10, you are now ready to choose an object. Place it before you on the cloth. You might choose a book, for example. Stare at the book, particularly to the side and top of it. Try squinting your eyes, or look at the book out of the corner of your eyes. You might stare at the book for a long time until, as it often does, your vision suddenly becomes blurred, at which time the aura of the book will probably appear.

Have trust in what you see, and allow your right brain to express itself without making left-brain judgments. Several things may happen when you are finished with the exercise. You may say to yourself, "But I have always seen that light and those shapes around things," and of course you have. Or you might decide that what you see is caused by your vision defects. Take your glasses off, if you wear them, and look again. You might decide you are trying too hard, and just imagining the lights and shapes around the object. These may appear to be lighter or even darker than the cloth background. You may also see the object very faintly repeated in exact shape several feet above. If you do not feel that you have seen anything special, never mind; your right brain hasn't found a way to tell you yet. It will work it out. When the timer rings, close your eyes and rest a few minutes.

Record all the things that you saw or felt in detail. Objects sometimes give off feelings.

EXERCISE 18
The Plant Aura

Set your timer for ten minutes. If this exercise follows exercise 16 by a few minutes, it is not necessary to pass again through the twenty-five minutes of preparation. If this is another day or time, then it will be necessary to do your preparatory exercises, so start with exercise 16.

Place a potted plant on the chair seat and look for its aura. This time, however, look at the tips of the leaves, along the stems, and at the end of growing branches. You will see a very faint green outline of a new leaf that hasn't grown yet, or just a faint green or other colored line around existing leaves. Sometimes you will see the outline (lower on the plant) of a leaf that has fallen off. Do the various types of looking mentioned in exercise 17 and look for other colors and shapes on the background cloth. Halfway through, turn the plant around and study the other side. When the timer rings, close your eyes and rest a while.

Record your impressions and the movements observed in detail on your tape. Since the plant is a living object, it might have reflected the energy you were sending it as you were looking at it.

◇   ◇   ◇

During the days that follow, continue the exercises using objects from around the house. You might include the seashell and fruit you used before. When you finish these exercises they should total several hours of work.

Thoughts are things. They are made up of energy. The air is full of thoughts flying around, and sometimes the thoughts stick on walls or objects near the person who is thinking. It is not difficult to prove. On occasion you have probably gone to visit friends unexpectedly, and the minute you walked into the house you knew that they had just had an argument, or received bad news, even though they were very cordial and apparently undistracted. Because of the intensity of the emotions involved, it had been easy for you to feel it. Here's another example that thought forms exist. Have you ever left the kitchen to go down to the cellar for some item, only to get there and discover you've forgotten why you came? If you return to the kitchen area where you had the thought originally, you will pick up on the thought form you left there and remember what you went to get.

The exercises that follow will help you pick up much more complicated and subtle thoughts—even events that have taken place long ago, and the people who were part of those events.

It is not difficult to learn about an artist by studying the thought-form aura around his or her work of art. We are not looking for obvious information, such as the fact that the artist uses bright colors with broad brush strokes; therefore he or she must be young or at least vigorous. We are looking for the artist's deepest feelings about self, family, friends, even sounds that are typical of the environment; the climate at the time the painting was done; the period and influences on the painting; the people who meant a great deal. This skill is called psychometry, or object reading. On every object is deposited information about its maker, its owners, its uses, and where geographically it was made and used. The invisible energy that gives you this information is not the same as the visible aura, but rather an invisible one which is more multidimensional. The two tend to overlap, though.

Objects for these exercises should be borrowed or recently purchased so your knowledge of them does not interfere with your reading. If they are borrowed from a friend, it is important that you record your impressions on tape while you are reading the objects, in order to verify your accuracy with the owner. Ask your friend for objects that are difficult to recognize in function and source. This makes the exercise much more difficult and exciting. Even better, ask your friend to wrap the objects in tissue paper—like gifts. In this way, only your right brain can participate in the exercise. You might tag the wrapped objects with a number and refer to them when verifying with your friend.

EXERCISE 19
Psychometry

Set your timer for ten minutes. Place the object you wish to psychometrize on a dark cloth on the chair. Follow the same procedures as before, again with your eyes open, at least from time to time. You may wish to do this exercise with your eyes predominantly closed, just checking from time to time. Use, in this case, your mind-screen to see things about the object. You may also wish to keep your eyes closed all the time and let your speech ramble on without being too much in control or aware of what you are saying. Each of us finds the method that best suits us. Record your findings as you go.

In the beginning, you may only pick up a few things about the objects that relate to them. Don't be discouraged; just give your left brain time to figure out how to be still during this thought process. As you progress, your skill will improve and your readings will become much more comprehensive and multi-dimensional.

As thoughts or images come to you, check yourself constantly for you will catch yourself changing or modifying right-brain hunches or feelings. Later when you check with the owner of the object, you will find that the hunch was correct, but what you did to it made it incorrect. The sooner you gain control over left-brain interference the better. When you do, many exciting things will come to you from the right-brain. You will also be able to discern between left and right brain thought patterns; their qualities are different.

When you become more sensitive to thought-forms on objects, you will also be sensitized to people and places. Stores, restaurants, gas stations, and banks will become study objects as well. From the aura of these places you will be able to understand employee work attitudes, the business financial status, and degrees of honesty in dealing with clients. You will have hunches as you enter these businesses. Follow your hunch if it is negative and walk out or drive away. (If you have to explain yourself, you can always say that you were looking for someone.) If you do not follow your hunch and decide to do business anyway, inevitably you will regret it.

As you open more, you will begin to differentiate between colors of auras that will express the current mood or feeling of the person you are observing. You will note that colors change all the time as thoughts pass through the mind. There are certain colors that will consistently designate certain moods and feelings, such as anger, fear, jealousy, pain, joy and spirituality. In our language we have wonderful explanations of meaning of colors. We say, "I'm blue" (navy blue), "I saw red," "I'm green with envy," "A purple passion" (deep purple), "He's in a black mood," "I'm in the pink." All these expressions are part of our daily language and, interestingly enough, are found in most foreign languages.

If you have difficulty seeing auras at first, here are a few suggestions that may help: turn your head to the side and use your peripheral vision to scan the aura. If you wear glasses take them off; squint your eyes until they are almost shut and try staring at the side of the head of the person until your focus naturally turns off—this could be the moment when the aura is very clear for you. When you go to church, temple or a lecture, study the speaker. This is often the first time you will see an aura.

In addition to the visible aura which offers information on current feelings, there is the invisible aura which can indicate recent events, the level of spiritual evolution, occupation and work setting, state of health, and finally an enormous collection of facts and feelings dating all the way back to the day of birth.

You will now be spending a great deal of time studying people you come in contact with, trying to interpret the many layers of the aura which surrounds them. Fortunately, the best way to look at the aura is to look at the temple rather than into the eyes, which demand a left-brain focus. You are less likely to offend than the artist who sits in public places making sketches. Whenever you find yourself where people are, practice listening to your hunches and admonishing your left brain for trying to interfere. It will be less important to verify your findings than to develop your intuitive right-brain seeing skills. You will know the feeling when your hunches are pure and correct, or when they sound fabricated by the left brain based on visual observations.

It is at this stage of learning that you must use the on and off switch in the right brain. When you are walking down a crowded city street, or you're at a party or other social occasion, you are very vulnerable to the powerful feelings of others. If these feelings were all positive that would be okay, but the anger, jealousy, rage, pain and guilt that people carry in their auras can be devastating after a while. Learn to protect yourself and when you go to a party, do the guests the courtesy of accepting them for the role they have created for themselves; accept them at face value—it's more fun for you and them.

In my groups on Becoming Attuned, the ultimate goal and final session is spent reading the human aura. Preparatory practice and final examination involve the reading of a mystery guest's personal life, in segments that include the date of birth to age twelve, from age twelve to twenty, and from twenty to the present. These periods were suggested by my right-brain as being appropriate. There are certain categories of questions you can ask yourself while reading the aura that suggest some order in the process, and also assuage the insecurity of the left-brain in the process. It is unfortunate that we are limited to the use of language, which we find more and more inadequate in describing the subtleties of the human experience. Here are some questions and categories you might wish to use as you practice using a friend or neighbor as your subject. These categories apply to almost all the periods selected:

1) Parents and close relatives: describe physical and personality characteristics

2) Homes and summer homes, homes of grandparents and relatives

3) Schools and teachers and special school friends

4) Toys, pets and favorite pastimes

5) Emotional concerns and problems

6) Serious relationships

7) Military history

8) Trips

9) Girl or boy friends; first dates

10) Adults who influenced your thinking on life issues

11) First cars

12) Scrapes with the law or authority

13) Career choices; first job

14) Emotional traumas

15) Sexual awakening

16) Illnesses

You will find that there is no logical order in the flow of hunches or ideas that come to you. It is therefore necessary to record or tape the information which is coming through.

When reviewing your findings with the subject, you will find that you are ninety-five to ninety-nine percent correct. Usually what your subject is not sure about is what he or she has forgotten. In fact, during your reading, memories of events will be dredged up and your subject may remember feelings that he or she has long forgotten. The subject may even have to check with parents to find out who is correct. You usually are.

EXERCISE 20
Aura Reading

Begin with exercises 5 and 6. Invite a new acquaintance (or someone whose background you do not know) to sit for an hour with you while you read his or her aura. Very few people can resist the temptation. Begin this exercise by going through exercise 16 (see page 57) using the two hands visualization. After you have completed it, open your eyes from time to time and look at the invisible aura of the person in front of you. Ask your subject not to comment or change facial expressions as you do your reading. Tape your observations and review them with your subject after you have finished the whole life, from birth to the present. Give your subject time to remember, as you list information you have picked up. It sometimes takes a few seconds for your subject to recall details of persons, or events that took place a long time ago.

After you have finished the exercise, ask your subject whether he or she has a friend who would like to volunteer to be read. Don't be embarrassed about asking near strangers if they would like to help you develop a psychic skill. You will never want for subjects.

When you reach a certain proficiency in reading auras, you will find that your right brain can record the aura in a few minutes. Sometimes you will see an aura, but it is not appropriate to "read it" when you see it. Your right-brain can keep it on file so you can do the reading later. Your reading will not be as comprehensive, but the general outline of the person's life situation (as of the present) will still be available to you. You can compare notes later with a friend (or that person) to check on your information, so you can further develop your skills.

If you work in a human services profession, these skills can greatly enhance the kind of service you can offer people. In traditional therapy or counseling, very often you can lead a client gently into recognizing and dealing with a traumatic past experience which is obvious to you, but which the client has successfully buried in his or her memory bank. This saves both the client and you time, and in some cases money, and encourages greater effort in dredging up issues that need to be dealt with.

It seems necessary to dwell a bit on words and their usage so far. Words are left-brain tools and tend to confuse people who are growing and developing spiritually. When I use the word "see" in the case of energy fields and auras, I do not necessarily mean that you see with your eyes. In my psychometry reading classes I often cover the object with a cloth before showing it to the group. This has in no way impaired their "seeing" or reading the invisible aura of the hidden object. When using the word "visualization," students often become blocked and announce that they are not visualizing or seeing anything on their mind-screens. However, when I ask if someone can imagine a past event between himself or herself and someone else, the reply is always, "But of course." So as hard as I try to select adequate words, someone will always give my word a personal interpretation and become blocked. If a word hangs you up, find your own substitute and don't worry—words have nothing to do with right-brain experience. One way to get over the block is to recall a scene in a movie or television program you have seen recently and then describe it out loud as if you were telling a friend about it. If you can, then you have visualized!

CHAPTER

8

Ego Trips and Traps

This chapter deals with a very serious subject. Quite naturally, you feel excitement and enthusiasm for your development, but you must also simultaneously feel a degree of awe and humility for what is happening to you. I'm not suggesting that you wear a hair shirt or chastise yourself regularly, but you do need to hold a constant and honest vision of yourself, including your spiritual rough edges, if you don't want to have your newfound skills "turned off." Who turns them off? You may never have to answer that question. Should you lose your reverence for these skills, or abuse the power that they give you, you will soon join the army of "has been" psychics who have not yet admitted to themselves that their source has been turned off. Probably turned off are those people who proudly and immodestly announce to almost anyone, at first meeting, that they are psychics. Proceed with caution when you meet these types. The question is not whether they are psychic or not, but how they use their abilities and for what purpose. I have met psychics who are miserable, lonely, self-hating people, who have found an ego-tripping opportunity to manipulate and fool others. They usually come on very "psychic" from the first meeting.

They see things, or read your voice and tell you how in one of your past incarnations you were a powerful prince or perhaps even Cleopatra. Cleopatra's soul must have been cloned into a thousand pieces, considering all the people who have reported having readings where they were told they were the reincarnation of Cleopatra! One wonders what would happen if they were all locked up together in one room. Would the true Cleopatra step forward?

Back to the "turn off." The turn off does not have to be permanent, but you must make a lot of Brownie Points before getting your skills back. Here are some of the danger signals which you need to watch for in yourself:

1) You go around with a half smile on your face as if you held a special secret.

2) At first meeting, and sometimes immediately upon meeting, you give a thumb-nail diagnosis of the person's current aura.

3) You become the life of the party, the center of attention, not by leading a quiet conversation, but by showing off your newfound skills. Instead of being satisfied with the attention of people who might be naturally interested, you seek the attention of everyone present. You haven't learned a very useful truth, *i.e.*, if you wish to meet interesting people at a party, who share common concerns, just find a spot where no one is sitting, and sit there thoughtfully sending out the thought-form of the subject you wish to discuss. Very soon a group of people will have gathered around you, and the conversation will inevitably be stimulating.

4) You begin to speculate on how to gain financially from your skills. This is the killer! If you give up your means

of earning your living, and decide to try to survive on your earnings from your psychic skills, that's okay, providing you are convinced you have something special to share, that you begin in a modest way, that you maintain a low profile, and that you always have time to work with some people at no charge.

5) You find that you are able to manipulate people who are close to you by "reading their minds" and jumping to conclusions even before they have had an opportunity to finish what they were saying.

6) You make quick judgments about people's physical and emotional health, and share your ideas with them, whether they wish to hear or not.

These behavior patterns are obviously extremes, and are not those of highly spiritual people, but when in a negative state, we can easily adopt them, if only temporarily.

The more you grow and learn—the more truly powerful you become—the greater the temptation to misuse the power. At this stage of growth, it is wise to increase the time and frequency you devote to meditation and contemplation. Frequent periods of aloneness are also vital to maintaining a balance. By remaining silent and alone you are better able to receive the wise and tempering counsel from your Higher Self, including easy doses of humility, which must go hand in hand with increasing spiritual power.

As you open up these new perceptions and skills, like a magnet, you will attract others who are having similar experiences and growth patterns. Often they may be just becoming aware of truths which you have already tasted. Resist the temptation to imply that you are already past that stage, or that, through your knowledge, you are able to speed up the process for them. There are no short cuts.

Everyone, consciously aware or not, is climbing to the top of the mountain; but at different speeds, up different paths, some more direct than others. This explains why you usually feel lonely on the path—it is only wide enough for one person at a time.

Another opportunity for ego gratification is to announce that you are a "channel" or medium. The temptation is great to pick a classic name such as Iseah or Sivarta and present this spirit as your source of truth. I wonder if naming these sources (and sometimes including a strong foreign accent during readings) adds greater credibility to the information coming through. Highly spiritual psychics, through their own connections, can deliver very wise and spiritual messages that can benefit many. With a little practice, each of you has the potential to channel truths and insights from your Higher or Soul Self, for your own information, preferably.

Beware of those who exploit people's fears and curiosity—the organizers of psychic fairs, those who set up free lectures in large hotels. Some organizers may be very sincere people, but there is no real need to popularize something that is already popular and available to everyone who is ready to learn.

In summary, the more you open, the more important it is to devote silent times to understanding, and at the same time to be reluctant to demonstrate smatterings of wisdom. Better to share your knowledge quietly with a single and receptive listener.

Using the Mandala and I-Ching

In earlier chapters silence and meditation have been described as means for receiving messages from your spirit guide or Higher Self or Soul Self. In this chapter, we offer you two ways of accessing your Higher Self that are more tangible and visible. The mandala is a non-verbal way of receiving energy and inspiration. Later in this chapter, you will learn how to use the *I-Ching*, which is an ancient Chinese oracle that has undergone many changes since its establishment about five thousand years ago, and which delivers a verbal, philosophical message. Both of these techniques can be extremely helpful in clarifying life situations, purpose and direction for you or others you wish to help.

The Mandala

The mandala is a universal symbol that has been used in all cultures over thousands of years. It is a design using the circle as its base. Often squares, triangles and figures are drawn within or slightly beyond the circle. The Tibetan sages design very intricate and sophisticated mandalas, using hundreds of god figures, flowers, and animals, which they use in their meditations and contemplations for enlightenment. The gods represent the forces of the universe—change, power, growth, understanding and more. The American Indians use the mandala in the form of sand paintings for various purposes, including a medicine wheel that helps a sick person heal. The famous rose windows that appear in cathedrals built in Europe in the Middle Ages are vibrant and intricate mandalas. The penitent knelt in prayer before the window and probably benefited from the glowing colors created by them. Color and shape are the most prominant aspects of the mandala.

The more you become conscious of the basic circular shape of the mandala, the more you see it repeated around you—in packaging and labels, as hex signs on Pennsylvania Dutch barns, in architectural design, hubcaps and medallions on automobiles, on fabrics, books and wood carvings, etc.

A great deal of research has been done and thousands of words have been written about the mandala. Carl Jung was fascinated by its symbolism and referred to it often in his writing. It is more important to understand how you may use it for your own purposes today. The mandala is a source of understanding and inspiration in reflecting the processes of your higher or soul self, clarifying your life purpose, showing you how others see you, and focusing special energy for physical and emotional wellness. However, it can deliver these messages only one at a time. Let's focus first on the aspect of color.

Science has demonstrated that color is reflected light, and that different vibrations of light produce different colors. But what science has not yet sufficiently investigated is how colors affect people, their moods and responses.

The colors you choose for clothing, cars and houses directly reflect what you are feeling in a non-verbal way.

When you begin drawing your mandala, it is better that you not become too preoccupied with the meaning of the colors or others' interpretations. Rather, choose your colors with no intellectual or even conscious attention. Don't take drawing your mandala too seriously. Enjoy yourself with magic markers. You'll probably chuckle as you find yourself sticking out your tongue as you did as a child when you were doing a special drawing. Before young children do representational drawings, they often draw mandalas. Try to recapture those childhood feelings of creative abandon and deep concentration. Imagine yourself listening to a boring telephone monologue while you doodle in color.

See the mandala as a great source of information and reassurance. It is the expression of your soul and your soul's energy message to you. Meditate on the mandala and become more wise. On the path you are taking to the top of the mountain, it is good to stop and rest every so often. Make the rest fruitful by checking to see how you are progressing. Draw mandalas as you progress. They will probably be different each time and will show you your progress.

If you are on a self-healing program and need a greater focus of energy to stimulate the immune system, ask your higher self for a mandala to use in your daily meditations. Daily contemplation of the finished mandala will be an integral part of your self-healing program.

◊   ◊   ◊

EXERCISE 21
Creating Your Mandala

Buy some wide- and narrow-tipped magic markers in a variety of colors. Use the wide-tipped markers to fill in larger spaces in your mandala evenly and the narrow-tipped for fine detail. You may also wish to buy gold and silver magic markers to add a certain amount of pizzaz to your mandala.

Use an 8 1/2 x 11 inch (or larger) sheet of paper. You can use a compass for your circles or whatever you have on hand, for example, a dinner and dessert plate to draw your circles, one inside the other. A third circle can be added. A ruler or straight edge can be used to draw triangles and squares within or extending just beyond the last circle. The purpose is to create sufficient spaces for filling in with a variety of colors. When you have completed the outlines of your mandala, take a few minutes to "let go" as the rest of the drawing is carried out without the participation of the left brain. When you feel that spacey quality of the Alpha state, which you experienced during your meditation, you may begin the second part of the drawing: adding color.

Spread your magic markers across the table and dreamily select the colors that seem to feel right. Put the rest aside and pick your first color and fill in the space that calls for it. When all the spaces are filled or when you feel that it is complete, pack up your drawing materials and tack your completed mandala up on the wall. Don't try to interpret it intellectually or verbally; just feel, as you stare at it, that the colors are entering you as you breathe in and are causing positive changes in you.

Whenever you get a hunch to draw another one, do so. If you are facing a crisis or need to be clearer about a situation, draw a mandala and have faith that it will help you.

The *I-Ching*

The *I-Ching,* or Book of Changes, is used extensively in China and the Western world today. Many have tried to explain why and how the *I-Ching* always has the right answers to carefully worded questions. Nobody knows why, but it works and its answers are appropriate to the situation.

In working with individuals and in workshops, I use the *I-Ching* as a means of receiving profound and helpful messages from the Higher or Soul Self. There are sixty-four pages of observation and recommendations in the book. Amazingly, they are written so as to respond specifically to whatever question you may have to present to your Higher or Soul Self. The Higher or Soul Self, in all its wisdom and experience, knows how the coins need to fall to give an appropriate answer, and makes them fall this way.

To ask the *I-Ching* a question, you toss three coins six times. For each toss, you draw a broken or solid line, depending upon how the coins are facing. Any coins will do; however, it is a good idea to use the same coins every time. The result is a pattern of six lines which then corresponds to a verse and explanation in the *I-Ching* book. Each page or verse has a keyword, such as "obstacles," "conduct," and "inexperience." In some books on the *I-Ching,* you have only a literally translated verse to read and interpret yourself. Other books do the interpretation for you, and in some cases, they provide specific statements for personal response and action. However it is presented, the sixty-four hexagrams (six-line combinations) offer deep understanding and precise direction in conducting yourself in situations relevant to the questions. In addition, the *I-Ching* will enlighten you about your personal and business life, inner development, relationships with others and challenges facing you in the near future.

The *I-Ching* can be extremely helpful in clarifying situations and suggesting future action. It helps you see the forest in spite of the trees. It often reminds you of what is already known, confirms a direction already chosen, indicates sensed patterns of future growth. Consult the *I-Ching* when some important event takes place and a decision is required. If you are a counselor or therapist, it will be invaluable in affirming a program of self-healing which has already been designed by you and your client. The more you use it, the more you will respect it and discover its ability to come right to the point. Keep in mind that the *I-Ching* should be treated with reverence and respect, and that questions are better thought out and written before tossing the coins.

EXERCISE 22
Working with the *I-Ching*

If you wish to consult the *I-Ching*, go to your spot, get into a meditative state and begin to write your questions. Ask one at a time on tape. Record the reading of the interpretation, the verse and keyword, using your own voice – not that of a friend.

Later, during one of your meditation periods, you can play it back again. Try not to write too many questions in advance, as you will find that the answers will lead to the next question. If you don't understand the answer you receive, you can ask for a clarification and toss another series of throws. As a result of the second interpretation, you will be much clearer on the first.

◊　　　◊　　　◊

In trying to understand the process of tossing coins and its direct relationship to a question—whether the question concerns the past, the now, or the future—you have to find a way to still your left-brain demands for logical and reasonable answers. For this reason, I suggest in exercise 22 that you get into a meditative state before asking your questions. Instead of demanding to know "why" or "how" the *I-Ching* works, accept and listen. This is difficult because Western society has a need to be in left-brain control. This need has been the driving force behind the development of our technology and science. Any unknown becomes a challenge, and we focus on finding answers. The Eastern mind, on the other hand, accepts the unknown, reveres it, and acknowledges its potency. Eastern society allows for the fantastic.

In order to use the *I-Ching*, you need to accept one truth, that you and the universe are one. If this is so, universal knowledge and truth must be available to you and everyone else. Events that have taken place, that are taking place, or that will take place anywhere in the universe have a direct effect on who you are and how you think and act.

How the coins fall when you use the *I-Ching* is ultimately controlled by you on an unconscious level, so the coins reveal to the conscious mind information that the higher self or soul already knows. This information offers you a perspective on yourself that relieves you of the need to react to every event in life as if your life depended upon it. It actually allows you to detach yourself and rise above isolated events. It can be used to provide a vision of yourself in a different continuity and can help clarify the meaning of true wisdom.

Both the *I-Ching* and the mandala exercises clearly indicate a need for discipline, clarity of purpose on our path. Both will help you on your search for self-awareness.

CHAPTER

10

Healing Opportunities

In the last few years, the word healing has become more widely used and in a broader context than in the past. Spiritual or self-healing is no longer considered the work of religious fanatics and misguided crackpots. Even nursing schools offer courses in Therapeutic Touch developed by nurse Dolores Krieger. Norman Cousins teaches humanism to medical students at UCLA, and clinics such as the cancer self-healing clinic run by the Simontons in Texas are growing in number across the country. Bookshops have greatly expanded their sections on health and self-administered techniques for maintaining wellness.

The concept of holistic medicine has become familiar to the general public but is still espoused by relatively few health professionals. The young doctor or psychiatrist who discounts holism will in all probability not continue to practice until retirement age, unless he or she has a change in attitude. Today, the public is better educated in medicine and nutrition than ever before and is demanding more progressive medical treatment. Hospitals will eventually become more and more oriented to maintenance of good health through educational programs for patients, greatly improved nutritional standards for patient meals, and workshops to teach patients self-healing techniques which will permit them to participate in their recoveries.

I recently visited a child in the pediatrics ward of a large city hospital. Because of the terminal nature of her illness, the staff decided that they could at least increase her strength by helping her to gain weight. It helped the staff to avoid dealing with the issue of her death, an issue which most people go to great lengths to avoid. I visited this child on two occasions, both times when lunch was being served. I examined the lunch tray carefully before she began to eat. Both meals consisted of a sandwich made from ham and processed cheese between two slices of bleached white flour bread with the crusts trimmed off. The sandwich had no lettuce, butter, or mayonnaise in it, nor was any green vegetable present on the tray. Two limp and faded carrot sticks sat in a cup next to a plastic bowl of mashed potatoes. There was a glass of fruit drink (the kind that advertises *10% REAL FRUIT JUICE and 90% water, artificial coloring and flavoring)*, and for dessert there was a dish of artificially flavored vanilla ice cream. Enough said.

We become so intimidated by the aura of starched efficiency, giant strides in research, several million-dollar cat-scanners, and intricate life-maintenance appliances that we are afraid to question any prescribed procedure or medication. We sit in a crowded doctor's waiting room, on time for our appointment, often waiting an hour or more to get to see him or her. When we do, we either forget or do not wish to "bother" the doctor with questions that have direct relevance to our illness. We just sit meekly and mumble, "You're the doctor. Thank you, doctor," as we leave with a new prescription.

A more satisfactory way to deal with the doctor and a way to get a better return on your investment is to take a list of questions with you and ask for answers—and write them down. Reassure the doctor that it is okay with you if he or she doesn't know all the answers, but to *please* say so.

There is a well-known cancer surgeon at Yale New Haven Hospital—Bernie Siegel—who says that you are in good hands if you can call your doctor by his or her first name. By what name do *you* call your doctor? What name does he or she use for you?

One of the most disturbing elements of traditional medical or psychiatric care is the immediate dependency that is created between patient and doctor. In all fairness, I must point out that many people go to the doctor to seek out dependence because it is comforting not to have to do anything for oneself. Some of these people, however, can be persuaded to at least try to actively participate in their own recovery. It behooves the professional to challenge them, with enthusiasm and confidence. The medical track record would certainly improve and eventually malpractice insurance premiums might reduce, if the responsibility for getting well were shared.

The other dependency, which is much more dangerous, is created by prescribing drugs, especially mood changing drugs, tranquilizers, uppers and downers. After years of dependence, withdrawal from some of these narcotics has in some cases been fatal.

The very personal experience of successful self-healing is a profoundly spiritual one, which can have a very positive effect on a person's future. Sadly, our orthodox medical treatment policy encourages dependency and the surrender of all control over the body at the beginning of medical treatment. The problem is due to the public as well as medical specialists' perception of treatment.

Many of us believe that even a comatose patient can take some responsibility for getting better at the urging of repetitive gentle persuasion. There are numbers of situations where a loved one or counselor has sat patiently by the bedside of a comatose patient carrying on a conversation of encouragement. It would be very difficult to prove, however, that this method is helpful in bringing a comatose patient around.

In the following pages we will talk about healing energy and methods, and we will set some patient goals.

Energy Centers or Chakras

Earlier we discussed energy sources and the process of storing energy in our bodies. In the East, these storage areas or energy centers are called chakras. There are seven such centers in the body (see figure 4 on page 32), which act like storage batteries for they build up energy reserves to be used by the body as needed. When a person is ill, the energy centers are low. The healing energy of a well person can be transferred through the hands to the ill person. This process may explain the miracles performed by faith healers.

In a well person, an equal amount of energy is stored in all the centers. When a person is ill, fatigued, or has overextended, the continuity of energy between all the centers is disrupted. One of the first steps in working with a sick person is to check the degree of energy emanating from each center, and equalize it by holding one hand over the weak center and the other over the unusually strong center. At the same time you visualize and feel the energy flowing through your body until both centers feel equal again. The seven energy centers should be checked for imbalances. You should also check the general energy fields around the head and shoulders. If the energy fields are out of balance, hold your hands equidistant from the side of the head and then the front and back of the head, and feel the energy for imbalance. Reduce the side with more energy by making a sweeping gesture with your hand down and away from the head. Test again. It may be necessary to sweep more than once. After you have equalized the centers and fields, the person will inevitably feel much better.

EXERCISE 23
Chakra Scanning

Before you find a volunteer to work with, you'll need to learn where the chakras are. Figure 5 will show you the approximate chakra locations. Check your own centers if you wish, before working on anyone else. As soon as you feel comfortable locating the chakras, you can work on volunteers. Your subject should lie down (on a sofa or on the floor) and close his or her eyes. The subject needs to relax and breathe slowly and deeply for a few minutes. Now rub your hands together vigorously a few times to better sensitize them, and beginning with the center of the crown of the head, start your scan.

As you move into and out of the energy radiation, you will have one or all of several sensations: a slight tingling feeling, particularly at your fingertips; a radiating warmth, as if you had placed your hand next to a light bulb; or possibly a cool feeling. However you feel, you will note the differences between the centers and the body areas among them. No one in my groups has ever failed, after a little practice, to succeed in this exercise.

If, at first, you have difficulty sensing the difference, I suggest that you use a sweeping gesture beginning at least

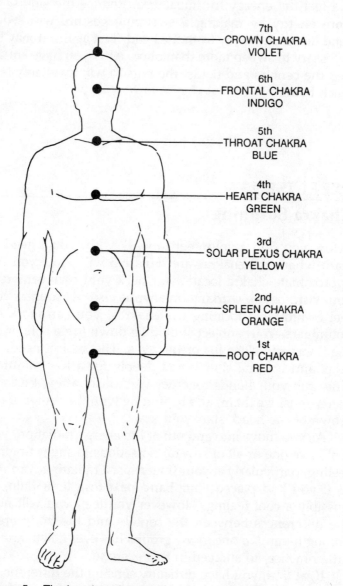

7th
CROWN CHAKRA
VIOLET

6th
FRONTAL CHAKRA
INDIGO

5th
THROAT CHAKRA
BLUE

4th
HEART CHAKRA
GREEN

3rd
SOLAR PLEXUS CHAKRA
YELLOW

2nd
SPLEEN CHAKRA
ORANGE

1st
ROOT CHAKRA
RED

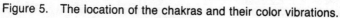

Figure 5.   The location of the chakras and their color vibrations.

a foot beyond the body and sweeping over the chakra and past another foot beyond, on the other side. Also make sure that you hold your hand about an inch to an inch-and-a-half away from the body. It is important that you be just as relaxed and peaceful as your volunteer; otherwise your energy will be out of harmony with the volunteer.

When you have scanned and assessed the centers, equalize them as earlier described. If you are right-handed, use the right hand to deliver energy and the left hand to receive it from the overly charged energy center. If you are naturally left-handed, then do the opposite. When it comes to equalizing the body fields, use both hands. Feel the overcharged chakra energy passing through your shoulders and down through your delivering hand.

Working with Color

For over a thousand years the chakras were visualized and used in Hindu and later Buddhist religious healing and meditation. The Buddhists developed a very intricate and subtle color pattern for each of the seven chakras. The Sufi sect of Islam later simplified this color system and still uses it for a special energy balancing meditation. Western culture accepted these colors and uses them in color healing programs. The colors we still identify with the chakras are shown in figure 5.

Today in Europe, the use of colors for healing physical, mental and spiritual disease is highly developed. We in the United States still characterize this healing as quackery. English language books on the subject are available in the United States from spiritual or New Age bookshops. I have used colored matte boards[2] to stimulate the healing process in children and also for encouraging positive spiritual change in adults. I suggest that you try your own experiments with color. Look over your wardrobe and note which clothes give you a good feeling and also the colors you wear when you want to be energized, serene, business-like, and so on. Then think about your favorite colors and how they affect your moods. Study the primary colors and, after staring at them for a few minutes, note your responses and feelings. You might begin with the "Sufi Color Meditation," exercise 24, and write down your feelings in your notebook.

EXERCISE 24
Sufi Color Meditation

Go to your special spot and get into a meditative state, breathing regularly and lightly. With your eyes closed, take a deep breath of red light and feel it gathering in your head. Hold your breath for a few seconds and see the red light begin to filter into all the cells in your head. Slowly exhale, with your eyes still closed and your head turned down, as if you were looking at your root chakra, which then begins to tingle as the red light spreads down your body and centers there. Repeat this twice with red light directed to your root chakra. Then move up to your next chakra—the spleen chakra—and use the orange color light. Every time you exhale the colored light, feel it reaching to the chakra and energizing it. Work your way slowly up to the crown, or seventh, chakra, this time sending the color violet upward into the crown.

---

[2]Available in art supply stores. Matte board comes in a wide range of colors, which is why I suggest it. Any colored paper will work just as well.

This meditation is very helpful when you feel the need to gain better control over yourself and a situation. It demands self-discipline and participation from the left-brain. It would be better described as a contemplation rather than a meditation. This meditation can be used to strengthen weak chakras in addition to the exercise you did earlier in this chapter, but in this case you add the color appropriate to the chakras. As the energy passes through your body and arms, you change its color to suit the receiving (or weak) chakra which you are trying to strengthen.

Healing Hands

The laying on of hands has been around since before the time of Christ. The technique has been traditionally practiced in the setting of organized religion and has just recently been accepted by hospitals as a beneficial healing technique. It can also work from a distance—people in "healing circles" project healing energy through their hands and focus on a person who is ill in some other place.

As with all instances of healing, there are two conditions that must be met before participating in a healing: First, the healer must be spiritually "clean," which means that he or she is free of dominating negative feelings such as anger, fear, jealousy, or emotional pain. These feelings can be projected and can be very destructive to the energy field of the person who is ill. The second condition is that the person who is ill has very clearly indicated a desire to be well.

There is sufficient evidence that hands have healing power; however, we can only speculate on what really happens. Certainly, low energy accompanies all illness whether it be physical, mental or spiritual. Getting better is usually characterized by having more energy. Focusing energy on the part of the body that needs healing *does* attract the attention of the natural healing forces within the person who is ill. This attraction is similar to the counter-irritant medical method such as the use of mustard plasters or capsicum ointment.

Placing healing hands over different parts of the body has a powerful effect on the healing process. One does not necessarily have to place them over a specific energy center but just in the area of trouble or pain. This transfer of energy can be done to others or to yourself. Take, for example, the healing of a common sore throat. One usually has ample warning before a real sore throat begins the process leading to a cold. At the first tickle or soreness, place your healing hand over the throat as often as you can during the day. Visualize healing energy flowing out of your fingers and palm and surrounding the inflamed tissue. You are helping the natural healing process to do its job. Don't be surprised when you wake up the following morning cold-free!

It is fascinating, when you think of it, how long you have been doing just this energy transfer without being conscious of it. When you have a pain or hurt yourself, your first gesture is to place a hand there. It always feels a bit better when you do. When you have a belly ache, you rub your stomach; when you have a headache you hold your head, and if it's a really bad one, you probably place a hand on each side of your head and transfer the energy through the ache. Although you have been doing this since childhood, now is the time to be more controlled and hold your hand in the pained spot for longer periods. And while you are doing this, visualize healing taking place in the area.

Rather than doing hands on healing for someone else, it is better to teach the friend how to do it. This avoids any dependency that could develop. When someone is very ill and weak, then a helpful treatment is justified.

Dolores Krieger, the Touch Therapist mentioned earlier, has found a way to be helpful to patients either in hospitals or at home. She uses three colors, choosing the appropriate color before laying her hand on the patient. If the patient is excited or frightened, she visualizes a soft blue-green light flowing through her hand into the patient to quiet him or her down. If you try it, you will be amazed at how quickly someone responds. If someone is low in energy, she sends a bright yellow light (the color of the sun and energy). If the patient is in coma, or the circulation is poor, she sends bright red light, but monitors the patient carefully to avoid overdose. Yes, an overdose of red could be harmful.

Keep in mind that healing should be taken very seriously. This energy you are using can be dangerous, but at the same time, it can save someone's life. Practice using it on your family and friends, but do it with reverence, and when you work with reverence, no harm will come to anyone. You may later decide to do some voluntary work in a hospital or institution where you will have an opportunity to transmit energy to those in need. Hands on healing is not the only way for energy to be transferred, however.

I must again emphasize that before doing any kind of healing on another person it is absolutely essential that you ask for permission. At the same time, be ready for a sudden change of mind. We must honor the right of a sick person to make the final decision whether to be sick or be well, or to live or die. You also need to ask your Higher Self for permission. You will receive the answer during a moment of silence.

Different Types of Healing

We have discussed one type of healing involving the transfer of energy from one person to the other, or by reinforcing your own energy in self-healing. The laying on of hands, a traditional and often religious activity, is increasing in popularity. However, the healings that take place in a crowd of expectant pilgrims at a shrine, or at the feet of a healer, may be only temporary. No research has ever been published, to my knowledge, on the duration of a miracle healing. My own informal research indicates that hysteria plays a part in the cure. Treating the symptom without considering the cause or the benefits of illness only postpones the total cure, and creates a euphoria which will inevitably end painfully.

A type of self-healing that is producing very exciting and tangible results combines meditation and creative visualization. The meditation creates an Alpha state at which time the right brain, where the healing process must originate, is most open to suggestion. This is followed by a visualization using symbols and images to deliver the non-verbal message that the right brain prefers.

There are two schools of thought concerning the use and type of visualization. One states that the visualization should depict the actions of the healing or immune system in the person's body. The other school of thought recommends that the person visualize restored good health. I have found that both are ideal in combination, the first at the beginning of a self-healing program and the latter only for use toward the end of the program when the person has acknowledged that healing is taking place and progress has been clearly noted. The indication here is that all the forces of the body are at work and no longer need reminding.

Often, a prerequisite for this type of healing is a self-directed program of stress management, using exercises provided earlier in this book. You have to clear the decks before healing energy and the immune system can go to work without distraction. In this type of self-healing, a counselor trained in these techniques is essential at the beginning. The average sick person has the will to participate in his or her own healing, but often does not know where to begin.

CHAPTER

11

Functions of the Counselor/Healer

The most vital question to ask the sick person is: "Do you want to live?" "To live? Of course!" is the typical answer. If the illness is the kind that can be terminal, then it is important to get the question answered early on in the relationship, in order not to lose valuable healing time. This does not, however, eliminate the possibility for frequent changes of mind, particularly during low periods. Recurrences are common, as well as relapses, and these temporary setbacks must be addressed openly and honestly. These appear often when an important emotional issue has not been considered during earlier sessions.

In the first phase, three objectives guide the sessions:

1) Searching for causes of illness,

2) Identifying the benefits of being ill,

3) Searching for alternatives.

From the very beginning of the healing program, the healee (a term we will use from now on) must participate fully in the search for understanding the causes and benefits of the illness. The healee also searches for less destructive alternative benefits. A real partnership of trust, hope, and enthusiasm established from the first session is desirable. The search for the cause of disease demands honest assessments on the part of the healee. In some cases, though, it is almost as if the healee had been waiting desperately to tell all, but had not been able to talk to family, friends, or doctor about important issues.

Searching for Causes of Illness

Begin by making an inventory of external stress experiences for the period from six to eighteen months prior to the illness. Table 1, listing stressful changes, may be helpful. (See page 18.) The list is not at all comprehensive and must be supplemented by a discussion of relationships and dependencies within the family, immediate and extended, and with partner, lover, spouse and/or children. A simple diagram can be drawn that will help objectify the family environment to the point where the healee can see for the first time his or her role. Shared needs and exchanged accommodations are part of the assessment. How does the illness affect each member of the family and what attitudes has it engendered? For example, is your sister jealous, sad, distant? Does your spouse deny the seriousness of your illness, or is he or she devastated? Are you receiving unconditional love from your mother? Is your father angry because you are ill? Is your grandmother very worried about you? These are just some of the questions you need to ask. (See figure 6 on page 97.)

The second kind of stress to be considered is that which I call internal stress, which is caused by long suppressed emotions that have established themselves firmly in the right brain in the long term memory bank there.

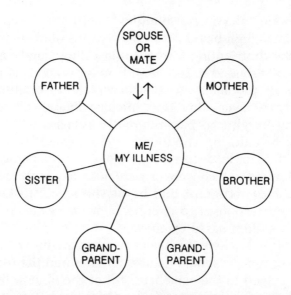

Figure 6.   How does your illness affect your family? This chart can help objectify relationships. The use of arrows can signify dependencies. An arrow pointing to the member means that he or she depends on you for support.

Efficient but self-destructive methods have been found by most people to hide or deal with these feelings. Alcohol and drug abuse are examples. The counselor teaches the healee the mind-screen exercise (exercise 4 on page 6). Suggest using this exercise frequently, until some of the burden is lifted. That which remains can be dealt with by the immune system throughout the course of the healing. Of course it is preferable to relieve the immune system totally, but the healee's need to cling to the emotions or feelings may be too great. The inability to forgive, particularly oneself, for real or imagined sins, is the greatest block to successful healing.

The next review or assessment must be made of past illness and a general medical history, which might include childhood sickness, allergies, asthma, hay fever, migraines, high blood pressure, arthritis, and so on. Discuss the contributing factors to past illness and how the healee progressed to recovery. Family reactions to old illnesses or problems are also important to discuss. Frequently the healee, in discussing past illness, will develop exciting insights to patterns and responses which were established during childhood and repeated throughout adult life. This leads to a discussion of the emotional needs of childhood, which were or were not adequately met. The healee may recognize that he or she is still looking for adequate responses to childhood needs. Adult relationships are often based on these.

It is vital to help the healee develop an understanding of his or her personality characteristics and the role that these played in the establishment of the illness. Be sure that the healee understands the difference between being blamed for the illness and taking responsibility for it. Cancer patients often become so enraged reading books on self-healing that do not make this distinction. So angry in fact that they refuse to participate in their own healing.

Some typical characteristics and behavior patterns that lead to life threatening illness include: always rushing to be on time, being extremely self-critical, a fear of failing, having a martyr complex, constantly looking for ways to serve others while denying own needs, constantly preoccupied with what others will think, and, finally, feeling guilty when doing something that's enjoyable or strictly for self-pleasure. Think of friends and family members who have had cancer and see if this description fits.

The use of the term "cancer victim" is disturbing. The term implies that there is a sort of conspiracy from the outside that attacks innocent people. The person diagnosed with cancer often says the same phrase over and over—"But why me?" The answer lies within. Cancer, like ulcers and other auto-immune diseases, begins because the immune or healing system in the body has been over-burdened by life-style or a series of stressful events that were beyond the control of the person. Many will dispute the theory, particularly those who have cancer and refuse to recognize their participation in its development. Once they accept responsibility, then they can also take respon-sibility for getting well. Research has shown, however, that healthy people also carry a certain number of cancer cells in the body, and these cells are constantly under attack from our healing system. So the cancer patient has a non-working immune system.

Directly related to personality is lifestyle. Although most of us have an idea of what is not good for us, we often live self-destructive lifestyles, putting off the reor-ganization of our life to a later date. You cannot postpone the permanent damage being done to your internal envi-ronment when you don't give proper care to your body.

The food you eat, a lack of structured exercise, the long hours you keep, the emotional extremes you enjoy, all take their toll and directly affect your future state of health. When a sudden and frightening danger signal hits, many people make all sorts of vows to straighten out. If you're lucky, the danger signal isn't fatal, and you are given a reprieve and another opportunity to treat your body as if it were your "temple."

Working with the concepts we have just discussed will take more than one session. In the interim, your healee should begin with a daily meditation program, without too many complicated exercises. The healee will then feel an enthusiasm from the beginning and a sense of hope. You may also wish to introduce the contemplative mind-screen exercise (exercise 4) early on, to deal with some of the chronic internal stress discovered during the assessment.

Identifying the Benefits of Being Ill

From a very early age we learn that there are benefits from being ill. As young children when we didn't want to do something, when we had not done our homework, or when we had done something which deserved punishment, we found that the best evasion was to get a "stomachache." As we became more skilled and in control of our right brain, we found that we could easily raise a degree of fever before having our temperature taken. We got so good at faking that we sometimes went too far and actually became uncomfortably ill, developing headaches, pains, stomach cramps and even vomiting. Even though parents and teachers thought we were faking, they also knew the futility of arguing over the authenticity of a headache or pain and consequently accepted and reacted as we had expected. In chapter 1 we discussed reactions and behavior patterns established in childhood that we still cling to today. The way we use illness as adults is not that much different; however, we seem to manifest more serious illnesses today.

In challenging the healee to list the benefits of being sick, we are inviting an angry denial and/or indignation. It is wise to question the benefits of illness at the end of a counseling session and give time for reflection overnight. Begin the following session by repeating the question. Assure the healee that we all have known the benefits of being ill, and that it is not a conscious process but a product of the right brain. Also suggest that in order to find more creative alternatives, we must become conscious of any benefits gained by being ill. Here are some of the benefits I often encounter:

1) We can withdraw from an untenable school, home, or work environment;

2) We can pass on a responsibility that we do not feel competent to handle;

3) We can avoid, or at least postpone, important life decisions;

4) We can gain love and attention;

5) We can get even with someone;

6) We can relieve our guilt;

7) We can avoid prosecution. (As children it was punishment.)

All these reasons, or a combination of some of them, are a dynamic part of every illness. Accidents, incidentally, are not excluded from this scrutiny. We almost always either produce them or participate in their creation. There are rare exceptions, however.

Searching for Positive Alternatives

After we are convinced that we have completed our search, we then move on to the more positive part of the exercise: the search for the positive alternatives to illness. Take a look at the list you have made together and make a plan for dealing with each "benefit." In addition to dealing with the specific benefits, you must add the two steps that are vital to recovery: building or strengthening self-esteem, and dealing with unexpressed feelings. If you have identified as one of the benefits of the illness the postponing of making an important decision, then the alternative might be to go to someone whose opinion you value and ask him or her to share in the decision-making. At this point the relationship between counselor and healee has become deeply dependent. Let it happen; as the healee begins to see signs of recovery, he or she will take credit for the change, and the relationship will reestablish itself on an equal basis. This may take some time, but that's okay.

It is at this point that the counselor and healee structure a program of meditation, visualization and contemplation. A stress chart (see figure 3 on page 17) is designed for the number one stress and assigned for daily use. The other stresses on the healee's list are charted in subsequent weeks. Contemplative mind-screen exercises continue to deal with internal stresses and unexpressed feelings, including those which surround the illness. I use a meditative tape, which allows time for visualizing the specific stress. The flip side of the cassette has two ceremonies visualized. In the first, called "Forgiveness," the healees forgive father, mother and finally themselves. The second, called "I Love You," visualizes an honest positive self-assessment before a large group of friends and acquaintances and ends in a declaration of self-love. These visualizations, repeated on a daily basis, begin to send a clear message to the right-brain which, in turn, gives the healees good feelings about themselves. As counselor, you might wish to tape the following visualizations for your healee. Better yet, ask the healee to tape them in his or her own voice. This makes the visualization more acceptable to the right brain.

EXERCISE 25

Forgiveness

You've come to the country for the weekend to see your parents. On a Saturday morning, as the cooling sun of fall approaches its highest point, you step off the front porch and walk along the gravel path of the garden, scuffing the yellow and orange leaves that have fallen during the night. You're not in a hurry; in fact you want to savor every moment of this very important day in your life. You enjoy the colors and smells of the chrysanthemums and petunias along the path, and you look upward toward the sun at the blue sky, squinting your eyes . . . and you see high up . . . a tiny speck, a hawk circling gracefully. You wish that you, too, could be as free as that hawk . . . but . . . perhaps after today you will know how the hawk feels. At the end of the long path, you turn right toward the lower meadow . . . and as you do . . . you hear distant choir music . . . and then you see it . . . down in the meadow . . . a stone amphitheatre with a simple stage in the middle . . . and in the amphitheatre sit many friends and acquaintances, nervous and expectant . . . and on the stage are three chairs . . . two occupied and one in the middle empty. As you approach, you recognize your mother in one and your father in the other . . . You climb the steps to the stage . . . pausing to nod to your friends. You look at your mother and smile . . . and you think . . . she's really a good mother . . . always did her very best to bring her children up properly. Sure, sometimes she made you very mad . . . particularly when she insisted that "it is for your own good," but then . . . she was usually right. She certainly gave her children plenty of love and attention . . . more than most kids' mothers. You feel a surge of love for her that you have never felt before . . . You turn to your father who is looking stern and uncomfortable, and you smile, trying to break the ice . . . You remember how many times in one day he used the switch on you . . . almost always when your mother reported that you had done something wrong . . . I guess that was the only way you knew him . . . a sort of executioner . . . You even thought he enjoyed beating you . . . but now you're not so sure . . . Perhaps he really loves you very much and never had a chance to express it other than by disciplining you . . . Your mother really forced him into the role . . . and maybe he is one of those people who have difficulty expressing how he feels . . . Guess you inherited that tendency . . . right? And then you begin to smile and he relaxes a bit. With a nod of their heads, your parents stand up and look at you, and in unison you say in loud clear voices: "The past is dead . . . It lies buried along with the pain . . . the anger and the jealousies." The audience smiles and nods as your parents sit down. They both look toward you, waiting. You look at your mother and feel warm, and you say in a gentle voice, "I forgive you, Mother." And then you turn to your father and smile at his discomfort, and you say in a louder voice, "I forgive you, Father." In the audience a few clap gently . . . You brace your shoulders . . . stand straighter and look up in the sky at the soaring hawk . . . and in a loud voice, you shout as if to the hawk . . . "and above all, I forgive myself." The audience cheers and rushes to congratulate you, but you take a second to look up at the hawk again . . . and breathe a sigh of relief . . . for at last you know what it is to be free . . . It is as if a great burden has been lifted from your shoulders . . . You turn and accept the greetings of your friends.

◇   ◇   ◇

EXERCISE 26
I Love You

You walk down the carpeted hall past the elevators and push through the leather doors to the ballroom. You hesitate for a couple of seconds, dazzled by the brightness of the large crystal chandeliers shining down on the crowd of formally dressed people gathered in groups . . . talking quietly. The men are in white or black tie, and the women in formal gowns, each holding a champagne glass which captures the reflection of the sparkling chandeliers above. You make your way slowly through the groups, hesitating at each, nodding and moving on. These are all friends and acquaintances from the past, and they smile as you pass and then resume their quiet conversation after you move on. Your heart beats faster as you realize that something very important is going to happen to you this evening. Suddenly the whole room becomes hushed as an old friend comes forward and takes your hand and leads you to the end of the ballroom. It is only then that you notice the low, red carpeted stage. Your friend leads you up the two steps to a white satin-covered cushion and signals you to kneel facing the wall of large drapes. As you do, the drapes part, and you find yourself facing a mirror, just as you do every morning of your life. In the mirror you see the crowd silently gathering behind you, waiting expectantly. But you are drawn to your reflection . . . you look . . . and you say to yourself, "You're not such a bad person after all . . . You're a good family member . . . capable of love and kindness . . . generous with your time and energy." You half smile, feeling rather good now. You look down for a second, and then stare again at your image and say, "You are a careful driver . . . hard worker . . . a generally honest person . . . of good morals, even." You pause, excited now, your heart beating faster, "You're not bad looking, in fact some would call you good-looking . . . Your skin is clear, and your eyes are bright, and your body is good, granted a little soft around the edges . . . but for your age that's to be expected." You catch your breath, and brace your shoulders as you realize that the most important moment of your life is about to come. You take a deep breath, blink your eyes and say in a loud clear voice, "I LOVE YOU!" For a few seconds, it's as if the world came to a stop, and suddenly there is a cheer from all your friends that have now gathered on the stage . . . and you turn around shyly as the band strikes up, and the trumpets blare, and the drums roll. Through the blur of tears, you take a glass of champagne and raise it high. You toast the world, you toast all your good friends gathered here, and finally you toast your newfound love.

◇　　◇　　◇

At first the healee will probably have difficulty in concentrating on the meditative exercises, and can at times feel that the whole effort is bound to fail. This is a natural response, as the healee has made a commitment to a process that is little known and often suspect. Suggest some of the exercises in this book, including the visualization of sitting in a circle of white sand. (See exercise 10 on page 50.) Be sure that the healee is breathing from the diaphragm and not only from the upper chest. When attached to a bio-feedback machine, people breathing from the upper chest only do not seem to dip into the Alpha state easily.

CHAPTER

12

On With the Healing

All over the country people are finding the miraculous effectiveness of using imagery or visualization to heal themselves. There is today enough evidence and documentation to satisfy even the most left-brain doubts. There are still a few hold-outs among the medical profession who find the possibility that a patient might be able to positively influence the outcome of an illness as threatening. Fortunately, these people are slowly being replaced by young professionals who are trained in a different way and are much more amenable to sharing responsibility for getting well with their patients.

When encouraging a person who is ill to use the techniques, the counselor must help that person understand the dynamics of the illness, the causes, the process that is taking place in the body and what the affected part of the body looks like. I use a full-color pictorial atlas of the human body. After studying the pictures and discussing the illness, we decide what needs to be done by the immune or healing system to bring about positive change. We then decide what elements of the system need to be part of the action. As a counselor, you need to keep abreast of new discoveries in the healing processes of the body, which appear in various publications and news-papers every day. Offer your healee the latest information available.*

One of the greatest miracles of the universe is the human body and brain and how they work together to maintain homeostasis, or balance, twenty-four hours a day. This balance is lost during illness, and the goal of the healee is to reestablish it. Once we learn the processes that are inherent in our bodies we will feel a powerful sense of of awe—and also a twinge of guilt as we realize how, for many years, we have assaulted it with poor nutritional practices and destructive lifestyles. In spite of these, it plods on doing the best it can. There are people who have never experienced true wellness in their lives and don't even know what it feels like. Often, it is healing from a serious illness that offers them this opportunity.

In the following paragraphs we will discuss the princi-ple elements of the healing process that will help the heal-ee design a self-healing program that will work. Under the general category of lymphocytes (white blood cells) are several varieties with special functions: the helper T-cell, which recognizes invasive foreign bodies, known as "Non-self" because they do not naturally belong in the body; the killer T-cell, which is then mobilized to eliminate them; and the supressor T-cell, which controls the response of the helper cell and keeps it from destroying normal cells in the body when the illness is cured. The proportional amount of these types of lymphocytes has been established for a well body. When the ratio gets out of whack, then we know that something is going on. Some researchers believe that a ratio of 1.8 to 2 helper cells to each suppressor cell is normal. When testing for AIDS

---

*A good reference for mind and body interaction is *Mind Matters* by Michael Gazzaniga (Boston: Houghton Mifflin, 1988). See chapter 12, "Healing."

for example, this ratio is studied and can help confirm the presence of the illness. Lymphocytes travel freely in the blood and through the lymph ducts of the body and are manufactured by the millions in minutes. The B-cell lymphocytes are the antibodies that are created to attack a specific "Non-self," whether it be a bacterium, microscopic organism, virus or allergen (allergy causing element). These also are produced by the millions, primarily in the bone marrow. Using these in a visualization will greatly enhance their activity and production.

Under the category of macrophages, visualization especially comes in handy; i.e., the phagocyte, which, like a member of an army patrol, travels the body constantly on the alert for the entry of "Non-self" invaders. Its task is to alert the healing system of the invasion, kill and eat the invader and collect identifying characteristics of the invasive organism which are then carried back to the antibody production areas where specific antibodies are made to deal with the invader. The "identifying characteristics" are like keys in that they are different for every invader, but are necessary as a means to "lock in" on the invader and destroy it. These characteristics are kept "on file," and antibodies continue to be manufactured and stored for possible later need long after the person is healed. Vaccination artificially introduces these characteristics and stimulates the production of antibodies, which are ready in case the person is exposed to the illness.

Pyrogens, from the Greek word meaning fire, also gather around the invader, primarily to assess the effectiveness of the healing process. If, at any time, it seems that the body is losing its battle, the pyrogen calls upon the hypothalamus, a gland which is in charge of the whole process, to make a fever, either localized or throughout the body. The purpose here is to raise the body temperature to a few degrees beyond what the invader can survive. When the pyrogen decides that things are again under control, it sends a message to the hypothalamus to end the fever.

Histamine causes swelling, which is an integral part of the healing process and is present to protect the rest of the body from toxins, dangerous bacteria and snake or poisonous insect bites. Reducing swelling after a poisonous bite, for instance, can be fatal in that the venom circulates too quickly and can cause heart failure or nerve damage. In a wound where dangerous bacteria multiply very rapidly under ideal conditions, the swelling protects the rest of the body from being affected too suddenly.

Mucous is an important element in the battle for wellness. It is primarily produced in our sinuses and when we are fighting a cold, will coat the mucous membranes of the throat, esophagus and bronchi. This is called a mucous blanket, and travels at the rate of two feet per hour down our throat to our lungs where it is coughed up and flushed down into the digestive tract. There is nothing wrong or repulsive about swallowing your mucous after you cough, and you are not necessarily making it easier for your body by spitting up. The mucous in your lungs carries dead bacteria, dead cells and tissue, histamine and fluid, all of which needs to be gotten rid of. I'm not sure whether your "used" mucous has any nutritional value, but it doesn't do you any harm.

Finally, understanding the benefits of endorphins and their role in the body can be helpful in making the healee more comfortable. The endorphins are our own morphine or pain killers. They also give us a constant, mild "high," which allows the nervous system to function relatively smoothly. These morphine-like chemicals coat the synapse (or arms) of message and pain neurons, which carry information to the brain. When the healee wants a break from the pain accompanying the illness, a color suggesting pain killing can be used in the visualization or picture. After severe injury, endorphins go into action immediately to dull the pain and make it less traumatic. Concentrating on an increase of endorphin production while in the dentist chair, for example, can make a visit less uncomfortable.

Once the healee understands these processes, he or she is given a box of crayons and some good quality white paper. Suggest that the healee give the imagination free reign, and that the drawing to be used for healing need not be technical. Encourage the healee to make the drawing as personal as possible, and possibly animated in such a way to suggest confrontational action. For example, why not draw the healing system as animal-like creatures or soldiers locked in battle with an invader? Your healee will associate toughness and strength with certain types of animals or cartoon characters that need to be in the drawing. You will find that pacmen, mostly jaws with giant teeth, are often used. Be sure that endorphins are included if there is pain associated with the condition of the healee. When the drawing is finished (and includes both the illness and the desirable healing process), ask the healee to describe it in detail. This imprints even more strongly on the right brain the visualization that must be used in meditation and during free moments throughout the day. If the healee is in bed and unable to move around, then the visualization ought to be recalled at least three times a day, using fifteen minute meditations each time.

Almost every illness or disease has pain associated with it. One of the easiest things to do in the beginning of an illness is to deal with the pain and feel some control over it. This is difficult to believe, but it's true. When the healee has either reduced, or eliminated, the pain for periods of time, he or she feels encouraged and hopeful, recognizing that taking control of the situation is within the realm of possibility. In order to get rid of the pain, the healee must change his or her attitude toward pain and see it as an important component of the healing process. Suggest that the healee welcome pain as the rallying signal for all the forces of the healing process to congregate at the point of illness. There are several techniques for reducing or eliminating pain which you can share:

1) Use the countdown. Give it ten to one, and ask pain to flow out of the body, through the hands, feet, or out the top of the head. After the third try, the pain should be completely eliminated.

2) Analyze the pain in detail, describing the different sensations and its location and intensity. After the analysis, the pain usually reduces or disappears.

3) Have a conversation with the pain, asking it to go away for just a little while.

4) If the pain is in an extremity, visualize it going away while holding the hand or foot in a bath of ice water until it becomes numb.

5) Visualize placing your hand in ice water until it becomes numb, and then place it on the part of your body that hurts and transfer the numbness.

If, after the session on pain, the healee is still not able to control it, then it may be necessary to make a cassette tape for daily use, describing the positive function of pain and how attitudes can block and even intensify it. The tape will be a repetition of the discussion you had earlier with the healee, but it offers more reinforcement on an ongoing basis.

The next step in the counseling process calls for sharing some of the techniques you have learned earlier in this book with the healee. You can help the healee to establish a structured and participatory role for his or her Higher Self or spirit guide by using the methods found in chapter 5. Encourage the healee to "meet" at least once a week with this wise and loving friend and ask for an assessment of how the healing is progressing. The spirit guide or Higher Self will also make suggestions for modifying or adding to the healing program. After the weekly meeting the healee must make notes in a journal that can be referred to later.

Preparing for Surgery

In some cases surgery may be indicated. The healee must be convinced that it is justified and then plan to participate as fully as possible in the procedure. There are several stages in the process where this is possible. There isn't a surgeon who is so sure of success that he or she doesn't welcome some stroking and reassurance. In order for the surgeon to do the best job possible, give a vote of confidence during consultations and express total trust in the positive outcome. This stroking can begin before the operation and continue right up to taking the anesthetic. In fact a cheerful greeting to all the operating room staff, and a vote of confidence to them, will make them want to do a very good job. In his or her greeting to the operating room staff, the healee might ask them to refrain from saying anything negative with regard to the operation or the condition of the area of operation. Although the members of the operating team might not believe that the patient on some level responds to these discussions, the healee would appreciate their cooperation. Dr. Bernie Siegel, whom I mentioned earlier, whispers encouragement in the ears of his patients during the operation. He will sometimes sing to them as well.

A visualization that I have found to be very helpful to those of my clients undergoing surgery is called the Garden Walk. "As you are being wheeled to the operating room, imagine that you are walking down a garden path of white marble chips. It is a very long path, but you can see the end where there is a small gate, just like the one that you entered. All along the path are flowers blooming and as you pass them they nod and whisper 'good luck,' and encouraging words to you. You know that by the time you get to the gate at the end of the path, you will be in the operating room. You can also begin this visualization as you are being put under by the anesthetist. You will set a very positive and calm mood and will in all probability continue your visualization as a dream while under.

If the garden visualization doesn't appeal to the healee, then you can invent one together. The main purpose is to inspire confidence in the positive outcome of surgery, and reduce the fight or flee response that makes it more difficult for the immune system to avoid the trauma of surgery.

When the healee is returned to the hospital room, the very clear focus should be on getting up and walking around just as soon as possible. While recovering from surgery, a new visualization can be introduced to the healee. Help the healee visualize the multiplying of healthy new cells, replacing those that have been damaged or removed through surgery. I will often describe the cells as round and rosy cheeked, like shiny apples, multiplying by splitting in twos in bursts of enthusiasm. If the healee can take a few minutes from time to time to hold this image on the mind-screen, the healing will be very rapid, and the hospital stay will be shorter.

Working with the Family

The family of the healee can either hinder or enhance the progress of healing. In some cases, because of geographical distances, the family has no effect at all. In order to enhance the healing process (after being sure that the healee wishes to get well), the counselor may meet with the family members to create a strategy to bring positive efforts into play. The illness of a loved one can often cause family members to feel angry, depressed, and powerless as they watch the healee deteriorate. Whether the healee is confined to a room in the home or the hospital, heretofore unexpressed feelings are bound to surface. Jealousies between members, resentments against perceived favoritism, feelings of inadequacy to deal with running the home, all create an energy that is negative and destructive to the healing process. Unconsciously, members carry their bickerings to the sick room and cause the healee to wonder whether he or she even wants to return to family life. In cases like this, I have recommended that the healee visit a distant relative for a few weeks in order to complete the recuperation.

When a healee is taken to a hospital, especially into an intensive care unit, the family suffers a crisis. Health professionals and doctors completely take over the healee, leaving very little for the family to do. The intensive care unit's philosophy seems to be geared toward the assumption that the patient is no longer able to heal him- or herself and that all vital functions must be taken over by mechanical means. This usually includes oxygen masks, which prevent the patient from speaking to family members; heavy narcotics, which make the patient sleep in a noisy environment; intravenous feeding, so that special treats brought by the family are forbidden. Restriction of visitation—both in number of hours and friends—isolates the patient and family members become confused, disheartened, and worried as they lose touch with the healee. They soon develop feelings of guilt when they visit, as if they were interfering with the professional care upon which the loved one's life depends. They whisper little questions to the nurses, looking for reassurance, and are reluctant to search out the doctor for answers. Doctors and nurses are overworked these days. The visitors are often brushed aside or asked to leave in order for some test, connection or disconnection of tubes to be made. The air of cool professionalism is intimidating and one gets the impression that if the hospital had its way, no visitors would be allowed. I have worked with healees in hospitals which, on the contrary, are homey and welcoming. These are the non-teaching hospitals, which more and more doctors are recommending these days. The atmosphere in this kind of hospital is more conducive to healing.

If the family feels out of touch with the situation, it is important to help family members feel that they are participating more directly in the recovery. I would suggest that the counselor call the family together for a discussion, allowing each member to express his or her deepest feelings with regard to the situation. As a counselor, you can only lead the discussion and suggest that there are ways to unite the family in a healing effort. Family, and even close friends, of the healee can agree each day at a specific time, wherever they might be, to take five minutes and sit in silence, visualizing the healee and the recovery taking place. Even friends and members of the family living in different parts of the country can participate in these healing sessions. Synchronize the time in order that all the energy is directed simultaneously. If this is not possible, then each person will choose the easiest time for concentration.

The healee feels guilty for becoming ill and causing such inconvenience to the family and to the hospital staff. There is the guilt of the family, for some members may feel that their behavior patterns may have contributed to the illness. Family members also feel guilty if they do not make frequent visits to the healee, and for leading normal healthy lives on the outside. These feelings must be brought out and discussed freely.

Plotting a New Life

During the process of working on a self-healing program, and especially after wellness has been achieved, the healee will learn a truth: that the quality of life is far more important than the quantity. The healee becomes highly sensitized to the natural beauty of the environment, learns to rejoice in the moment and to give unconditional love. When the counselor senses this new awareness, it is time to help the healee make plans for the future, to plan for the day of recovery, and build a life image with a new set of values as guidelines.

In past conversations with the healee, the counselor will have picked up bits and pieces of information which can be helpful at this stage. A discussion of the "old" lifestyle, relationships, use of leisure time, and personal growth patterns will lead to some very creative decisions about the future. The support of the counselor is much needed as the healee makes decisions to give up the old— the known, and often negative patterns—to replace them with new, positive, and unknown directions. It is scary to blast away at the foundation upon which daily life is based, and try to replace it with a structure that we have only heard about and never experienced. Together you will find the process of choice and decision exciting and often fun. The severing of destructive relationships and unproductive life patterns will be painful—but essential—if a recurrence of illness is to be avoided. In order to meet new people and make new friends the healee may need to change churches, join a hobby group, take evening classes, change jobs, attend public functions, or even place or answer an ad in the personal column of a local paper. How often we have heard the statement, "I often wish I had taken up water coloring, or rock hunting, or white water canoeing, the guitar, or square dancing." All this is available to the public and offers the healee an opportunity to meet people who share the same interests.

During this process, emphasis must be placed on the need for the healee to make decisions for change without consulting family members or loved ones. The healee must recognize that planning a new life is not a selfish process, and that decisions to change will not seriously disrupt or adversely affect the basic structures of the family. This will be very difficult if the healee is one who serves others and denies personal needs. The personality profile of some cancer patients is one with an excessive desire to serve others, to sacrifice for others, to deny personal pleasure or satisfaction. Naturally this type will feel guilty when asked to plan for the future without considering the reactions and needs of family members and friends. The counselor's role here is very clear. He or she must for the first time exert pressure, and insist that the healee begin the process of change and deal with the guilt feelings at the same time. Unless these feelings are dealt with, a recurrence of the disease is inevitable, and the healee will sometimes give up, and in some cases, choose to die. Death sometimes seems to be easier than saying "no" to others—or putting your own needs before someone else's.

The counselor must aid in maintaining a line of open communication between the healee and loved ones. If communication has been non-existent for some time, the healee will need to reestablish it, including the capacity to say "no" without anger or guilt. This is an important stage in the healing process and in safeguarding against an illness recurrence. If the reopening communication is difficult for the healee, the counselor may suggest that writing a long letter to another person may be a more comfortable first step.

If the healee has decided to live, goals need to be set for the immediate future. These new goals should be within the capacity of the healee as failure would be disastrous at this stage. Taking the step is more important than the goal itself. One goal might be having a good talk with a loved one—a family member or friend—in which honesty is the priority. Or the goal might be making inquiries of evening courses taking place in the community, planning a short trip, joining a bird watching club, learning needlepoint, searching for an old friend with whom the healee has lost contact, planning a new hairstyle. All these have one common and very important ingredient: they indicate that recovery will take place and that it is safe to make specific plans for the future.

The euphoria that often follows a recovery is dangerous in that it can be a first step to recurrence of the disease. Therefore, the new life plan must encompass a strict and structured program for wellness maintenance. The healee will need to study nutrition. By reading and consulting and by the trial and error method, he or she will learn to develop a diet that is comfortable and supportive of a high level of wellness. The trial and error method is the most reliable and involves withholding certain food types from the diet for four to five days and then on the following day to begin eating the food again. By making notes on how the healee felt during the period of withdrawal and after resuming the food, the healee can soon, after running through several types of food, establish a workable diet. Withholding foods that are craved is another part of the testing. Foods that we crave are often foods we are allergic to. Once a diet has been established then a program of regular exercise becomes part of daily life. Exercises that are chosen must be within the limitations of the healee and not cause unnecessary strain or tissue damage. Meditation and creative visualization must become just as much a part of the daily routine as brushing one's teeth. And finally, a time for reading must be available to learn more about the field of healing and life management.

Afterword: A Beginning

Well, dear friend—we must be friends by now—how does it feel to be powerful? I am grateful that you have reached this point, because I know how you are feeling about yourself. You are bursting with energy, overflowing with a kind of religious fervor, wanting everyone to have the same experiences and feelings. You are ready to help, I know. That is how you will continue to grow, and there's a lot more growing to do.

Your mission goes beyond those people in your closest orbit and out into the world society. Raise your spiritual aura on high! Be ready always to encourage and support spiritual transformation in others. Help them to feel balanced and integrated, at peace with their internal environment, and to taste the true meaning of power. Encourage individuals to take responsibility for their lives, actions, and wellness.

Crime, violence, and battle are symptoms of low self-esteem and a feeling of powerlessness. Individuals, groups, and nations can feel this way. Boredom is another symptom when people feel no control over daily events. Their solution is to escape by creating emotional and social violence in their lives or in the lives of family and friends—starring in their own soap operas and drawing others into their negative emotional voyages.

If you want to become powerful, you need to find a way to break into those patterns to offer a positive alternative. Setting an example with the way you lead your life is commendable, but much more needs to be done. When the opportunity arises, challenge people's values and priorities, point out missed opportunities, discuss the benefits of mind, body, spirit integration; and above all, shower the people you meet with unconditional love. And when a timid hand reaches out to you, grasp it firmly and lovingly.

Write me and tell me of your experiences and feelings. I will answer as I would to a friend—honestly, caringly, and probably after quite a while.